Advertising and Consumption

This book argues for the study of consumption and its relationship with media images, particularly advertising, from a cultural perspective. Focused on Brazil, it draws on decades of research by the author and engages with theory and concepts from a range of classic anthropological works. The chapters examine how advertising professionals view their craft, the resistance to capitalism amongst native Brazilians, images of women and their bodies in magazines, and the case of the first soccer player to become a national media celebrity. Rocha supports the study of consumption as a classification system that materializes culture and creates relations between people and goods. The book presents advertising as a mode of magical thinking that mediates the passage from the machine-driven sphere of production to the humanized sphere of consumption, converting meaningless impersonal things into goods that have name, origin, identity, and purpose. It will be of interest to anthropologists, sociologists, and others working on advertising, marketing, communications, and consumer research.

Everardo Rocha is a Full Professor in the Graduate Program in Communication of the Department of Social Communication at the Pontifical Catholic University of Rio de Janeiro (PUC-Rio), Brazil. He received his PhD in Social Anthropology from the National Museum, Federal University of Rio de Janeiro (UFRJ). His research has the support of the National Council for Scientific and Technological Development (CNPq) and the Carlos Chagas Filho Foundation for the Support of Research in the State of Rio de Janeiro (Faperj). Everardo Rocha is author of numerous books, edited volumes, and articles on the anthropology of consumption, advertising, and Brazilian culture.

Anthropology and Business
Crossing Boundaries, innovating praxis
Series Editor: Timothy de Waal Malefyt

Both anthropology and business work at the forefront of culture and change. As anthropology brings its concerns with cultural organization and patterns of human behavior to multiple forms of business, a new dynamic of engagement is created. In addition to expanding interest in business as an object of study, anthropologists increasingly hold positions within corporations or work as independent consultants to businesses. In these roles, anthropologists are both redefining the discipline and innovating in industries around the world. These shifts are creating exciting cross-fertilizations and advances in both realms: challenging traditional categories of scholarship and practice, pushing methodological boundaries, and generating new theoretical entanglements. This series advances anthropology's multifaceted work in enterprise, from marketing, design, and technology to user experience research, work practice studies, finance, and many other realms.

Titles in series:

The Magic of Fashion
Ritual, Commodity, Glamour
Brian Moeran

Women, Consumption and Paradox
Edited by Timothy de Waal Malefyt and Maryann McCabe

Advertising and Consumption
Anthropological Studies in Brazil
Everardo Rocha

Digital Cultures, Lived Stories and Virtual Reality
Thomas Maschio

For more information about this series, please visit: https://www.routledge.com/Anthropology—Business/book-series/AAB

Advertising and Consumption
Anthropological Studies in Brazil

Everardo Rocha

LONDON AND NEW YORK

First published 2022
by Routledge
2 Park Square, Milton Park, Abingdon, Oxon OX14 4RN

and by Routledge
605 Third Avenue, New York, NY 10158

Routledge is an imprint of the Taylor & Francis Group, an informa business

© 2022 Everardo Rocha

The right of Everardo Rocha to be identified as author of this work
has been asserted by him in accordance with sections 77 and 78 of
the Copyright, Designs and Patents Act 1988.

All rights reserved. No part of this book may be reprinted or
reproduced or utilised in any form or by any electronic, mechanical,
or other means, now known or hereafter invented, including
photocopying and recording, or in any information storage or
retrieval system, without permission in writing from the publishers.

Trademark notice: Product or corporate names may be trademarks
or registered trademarks, and are used only for identification and
explanation without intent to infringe.

British Library Cataloguing-in-Publication Data
A catalogue record for this book is available from the British Library

Library of Congress Cataloging-in-Publication Data
Names: Rocha, Everardo P. Guimarães, 1951- author.
Title: Advertising and consumption : anthropological studies in Brazil /
Everardo Rocha.
Description: 1 Edition. | New York, NY : Routledge, 2022. |
Series: Anthropology and business | Includes bibliographical references
and index.
Identifiers: LCCN 2021020697 (print) | LCCN 2021020698 (ebook) |
Subjects: LCSH: Advertising—Social aspects—Brazil. | Consumption
(Economics)—Social aspects—Brazil. | Consumer behavior—Brazil. |
Brazil—Social life and customs.
Classification: LCC HF5813.B8 R634 2022 (print) |
LCC HF5813.B8 (ebook) | DDC 306.30981—dc23
LC record available at https://lccn.loc.gov/2021020697
LC ebook record available at https://lccn.loc.gov/2021020698

ISBN: 9781032004648 (hbk)
ISBN: 9781032010212 (pbk)
ISBN: 9781003176794 (ebk)

DOI: 10.4324/9781003176794

Typeset in Sabon
by codeMantra

To my wife Ana Paula and our sons João Felipe, Antonio Pedro, and José Eduardo, for all their love and encouragement.

Contents

Foreword	ix
Acknowledgments	xi

1 Guilt and pleasure: challenges and possibilities for understanding consumer culture — 1

PART I
Perspectives on consumption through fieldwork experiences — 11

2 Totemism in the market: Lévi-Strauss as an inspiration for consumption research — 13

3 A tribe of white collars: bricoleurs in the business of advertising — 31

4 Against capital: the resistance to economic thought among the Terena of central Brazil — 53

PART II
Perspectives on consumption through media images — 75

5 The woman in pieces: advertising and the construction of feminine identity — 77

6 Classified beauty: goods and bodies in women's magazines — 100
WITH MARINA FRID

7 A star player in the world of goods: marketing and the first Brazilian soccer celebrity — 119
WITH WILLIAM CORBO

Index — 137

Foreword

What are we to make of the terms advertising and consumption? Are they possible windows into a culture and to the values of a society? Are they a way to read and interpret a local repertoire of consumer behavior in a capitalist society, whereby marketing and advertising efforts ostensibly underpin economic growth by enlisting citizens into efficient consumers? On the one hand, they represent controversial terms in anthropology, carrying notions of unchecked consumer fetishism and privileged relationships between humans and things that might obscure more important relations between people. On the other hand, anthropologists, such as Daniel Miller (1998), claim understanding these terms is essential to uncovering meaning in the everyday lives of people in the contemporary world, because consumption, for one, underscores the implicit and explicit set of values in relations among and between people in the things they buy for others. It is in this latter sense that Brazilian anthropologist Everardo Rocha introduces us to the values, semiotic meanings, and structural relations that exist relative to these terms in Brazilian culture.

While anthropological studies of consumer culture and the advertising industry in different parts of the world have proliferated since the late 1970s, not much has been written on Brazilian advertising and consumption to English speaking audiences, to which this present volume addresses. Anthropologists such as Brian Moeran (1996) have provided a fascinating look at Japanese culture through the lens of its advertising agencies, showing the delicate work of balance and trade-offs in Japanese social relations that is played out among advertisers, media, and agencies. William Mazzarella (2003) shows us the work of advertising and consumption in India, where such processes afford a means for modernizing society, bringing Western culture to Indian people through images of alternative lifestyles. Timothy de Waal Malefyt and Robert Morais (2012) reveal advertising practices in the US from an emic perspective of work within ad agencies, revealing rituals of transformation and separation, impression management, and the various creative processes that bring high-level advertisements to ordinary people. Now, Everardo Rocha adds to the global study on consumer culture by providing a rich and detailed investigation of Brazilian culture through the lens of consumption and advertising. In a series of lively chapters, Rocha gives us a range of perspectives on Brazilian culture, posing such questions as how we might interpret the meaning of messages various advertisements bring to Brazilian people; how ad

x *Foreword*

agency representatives act as bricoleurs in assembling fragments of cultural knowledge already available in social thought; and how certain indigenous Brazilian communities, such as the Terena, resist efforts of marketing and consumption and avoid assimilation by opposing capitalism and asserting their impearled cultural identity. Rocha further compares the effects of advertising in the Brazilian beauty industry from the view of two historical eras: first during the 1980s when the women's movement in Brazil sought liberation and voice for women only to have advertised products "speak on their behalf" and express their needs, desires, and choices; then during the 2010s, when, along with colleague Marina Frid, he examines advertisements that relate to women's body image, health, and well-being using the logic of totemism that categorizes women's needs and desires. In a fascinating chapter, Rocha along with his coauthor, William Corbo, reveals how Leonidas da Silva, called "the Black Diamond," had a huge impact on Brazilian culture in the 1930s and the 1940s as the first global sports celebrity of Brazil. As a discriminated Black player, da Silva overcame racial tensions and became emblematic of Brazilian culture as an amalgam of opposites, capable of overcoming differences and divisions, to unite the best of different worlds.

Throughout Rocha's analysis in these chapters, we read how advertising and consumption are the very structures that act as refinements of and for civilization and become the means in Brazilian society in different eras for developing norms, values, and perspectives that bring new adaptive practices to society. But Rocha also draws our attention to the social and cultural implications of advertising messages that recognize the ways in which marketing ideology also coerces and masks power relations to promote, for instance, gender inequalities, as it also provides a means of acquiring prestige and value for select others. This book provides multiple examples of the systematic ways in which advertising and consumption work together to impact social structure as vehicles for highlighting and obscuring the social order of relationships among humans and the nonhuman world of objects, things, and nature. This book helps us understand Brazilian society and power relations through concepts of identity, gender, class, social group formation and resistance, and the value systems they express through the effects of consumption and advertising. From these views, we gain entrance into the workings of Brazilian culture, written with keen anthropological insight. Rocha's fascinating book is a pleasure to read that I hope many will enjoy, as I did.

Timothy de Waal Malefyt, Brooklyn, NY

References

Malefyt, Timothy de Waal and Morais, Robert J. 2012. *Advertising and Anthropology: Ethnographic Practice and Cultural Perspectives.* Oxford: Berg.

Mazzarella, William. 2003. *Shoveling Smoke: Advertising and Globalization in Contemporary India.* Chapel Hill, NC: Duke University Press.

Miller, Daniel. 1998. *A Theory of Shopping.* Cambridge: Polity.

Moeran, Brian. 1996. *A Japanese Advertising Agency.* Honolulu: University of Hawaii Press.

Acknowledgments

Writing a book is always an experience that we share with people and institutions that accompany us and generously offer their support, patience, and ideas. Whatever is best in this book, I dedicate to them.

In particular, I thank Professor Timothy de Waal Malefyt of Fordham University, editor of Routledge's Anthropology & Business series, for our intellectual exchanges and his invaluable support on this book project, from the initial proposal to the foreword he so kindly agreed to write. I also thank everyone at Routledge involved in the editing of this book, especially Katherine Ong, for her pertinent advice and assistance throughout the entire process. The proposal's reviewers shared precious feedback and ideas that contributed to this book as well. I dedicate a special thanks to the research interlocutors who offered their time, patience, and wisdom so that I could carry out these studies, particularly Chapters 2–4.

I am grateful for the constant support I have received throughout my career from the National Council for Scientific and Technological Development (CNPq), through its Research Productivity grant, and the Carlos Chagas Filho Foundation for the Support of Research in the State of Rio de Janeiro (Faperj), through its Scientist of Our State funding program. The support I receive from these Brazilian institutions dedicated to fomenting scientific research was decisive in the making of this book.

I thank the Pontifical Catholic University of Rio de Janeiro for being an institution I am proud to be a part of for more than 40 years. I feel very privileged to share a pleasant and intellectually stimulating work environment with my fellow professors and students of the Communication Department and the Graduate Program in Communication at PUC-Rio. Specifically, I would like to thank Professor Tatiana Siciliano, Director of the Department, and Professor Arthur Ituassu, Coordinator of the Graduate Program.

My thanks to the entire team of students and researchers who collaborate with the Laboratory of the Anthropology of Communication and Consumption (LACC) of the Graduate Program in Communication at PUC-Rio for the intense exchange of ideas and collaborations in several academic articles. I am grateful for the partnership of my coauthors in two chapters

xii   *Acknowledgments*

in this book – Professors Marina Frid of the Graduate Program in Communication and Culture at the Federal University of Rio de Janeiro (UFRJ) and William Corbo of the Institute of Philosophy and Social Sciences also at UFRJ – and of Professor Bruna Aucar of the Department of Communication at PUC- Rio, who shares the coordination of LACC with me. My special thanks to Professor Marina Frid, who was an essential collaborator in the stages of preparing the proposal and writing the English version of Chapters 1–4, besides offering valuable contributions to the improvement of the book.

I cherish the fond memory of my parents Rubem and Wanda Rocha, my brother Rubem Rocha Filho, and Professor Agenor Miranda Rocha, who are forever present in my life.

Finally, Chapters 5–7 are adapted and revised versions of previously published articles. I thank and credit the sources of the original works:

Rocha, E. (2013). The woman in pieces: advertising and the construction of feminine identity. *SAGE Open*. doi:10.1177/2158244013506717.

Rocha, E.; & Frid, M. (2018). Classified beauty: goods and bodies in Brazilian women's magazines. *Journal of Consumer Culture*, 18(1), 83–102. doi:10.1177/1469540516641625.

Rocha, E., & Corbo, W. (2017). A star player and the world of goods: soccer and consumption in the public image of Leônidas da Silva. *Sociologia & Antropologia*, 7(3), 799–823. doi:10.1590/2238-38752017v736.

1 Guilt and pleasure
Challenges and possibilities for understanding consumer culture

Consumption has an inescapable presence in the great contemporary metropolises. Elements like supermarkets, malls, shop windows, billboards, ads, delivery vehicles, and discarded cardboard boxes are so pervasive that it is easy to take them for granted. I argue, however, that consumption and its accompanying discourse, advertising, warrant attention. After all, along with production, consumption is one of the necessary pillars of modern capitalism. As a phenomenon of culture, consumption reveals and produces symbolic maps: it attributes values, structures practices, regulates social relations, and defines identities. Hence, to understand "consumer culture," systematic studies, interpretations, and theories are necessary.

Despite its significance and complexity, consumption was for long not a prominent focus of the social sciences. Compared to investigative efforts that turned to production and used it as a path for explaining modernity, dedication to consumption was rather shy, at least until the late twentieth century. Why would such a fundamental phenomenon in industrial societies not be at the center of sociocultural debates?

The hesitancy and shyness that for long hampered more prolific and systematic reflections about consumption – and that, to a lesser extent, still does – is in itself meaningful, revealing much about the modern Western ethos. Certain ideologies surrounding the issue of consumption obstruct and obscure research possibilities. It is as if everyone has precipitated views, feelings, and judgments about consumption because it is something that most people, one way or another, experience in capitalist contexts.

Admittedly, this kind of problem is not new. Freud referred to it as well as the greatest challenge to building a psychoanalytic theory. Because everyone has psychological processes, everyone thinks they know about the psyche. The same happens with the concept of culture. As many anthropologists have discussed, the shared experience of culture is different from a theory of culture. In the preface to his *Apocalittici e Integrati*, Umberto Eco also attributed the difficulty in discussing the "cultural industry" to the excess of ideas attached to the expression. All of this means that emotional and ideological views tend to obfuscate themes more than they contribute to

DOI: 10.4324/9781003176794-1

2 Guilt and pleasure

methodical investigations, consistent reflections, and the development of solid theories.

Shedding light on common biases that tend to inhibit or limit the debate is a strategy to nurture persistent and solid advances in consumption research. These biases are present in informal conversations, media representations, and some fields of academic and technical knowledge. Over my decades of experience studying advertising and consumption, I have identified diverse meanings ascribed to consumption in what tend to be hasty or simplified explanations of the phenomenon. I summarize these meanings in four principles – hedonism, moralism, biologism, and utilitarianism. These are not mutually exclusive principles that often bias attempts to explain consumption.

Throughout my academic career, I sought to overcome these biases and contribute to nuanced and deep analyses of advertising representations and consumer experiences as central issues for understanding modern-contemporary societies. *Advertising and Consumption: Anthropological Essays* presents my cultural approach to investigating advertising, consumption, and the symbolic properties of goods established through ads and other media images in six essays that draw from over 40 years of research. Based on anthropological theories and methods, essays explore consumers' interpretations of advertising, the views of ad professionals over their craft, the resistance against capitalism of an indigenous people of Brazil, representations of women and their bodies in magazines, and the case of a soccer player turned into media celebrity in the 1930s on the eve of the expansion of the sports industry.

By way of an introduction to these essays, I propose first to expose and deconstruct biased perspectives on consumption that persist even today, despite advances in sociocultural studies on the phenomenon. I will make a kind of inventory of the most common uses of the term "consumption" to discuss what these definitions reveal and conceal. Resisting and breaking from hedonism, moralism, biologism, and utilitarianism must be a constant and conscious exercise for researchers who want to comprehend consumer cultures, so ingrained these principles are in modern Western thought.

***

The ideological marks that most often intersect discourses about consumption, hindering deeper analyses, are reductionists in different ways. Though these ideological biases usually emerge together, in various combinations, I will address them separately for didactic purposes, starting with the mark I call hedonist.

The hedonist mark sees consumption through the prism of advertising. Perhaps that is why everyday discourses so frequently identify consumer practices as hedonistic. As a rule, mass culture thinks about consumption through an ideology that equates possession of goods to happiness.

Guilt and pleasure 3

Alcoholic beverages connect beautiful and fun people, cars materialize and display personal achievements, cosmetics protect, rejuvenate, and seduce. Products and services conspire for our perennial well-being and pleasure. It is as if consumption were like a passport for blissfulness. Advertising is the official voice of the hedonist mark.

Hedonism is the mainstream ideology of consumption, so to speak. It is the most recurrent and emphasized in the media, above all in advertising. Commentaries swayed by the hedonist principle frame consumption as a pursuit for pleasure, a matter of individual choice, taste, and desire. In other words, the hedonist view ends up reproducing or agreeing with advertising persuasion.

The pervasiveness of the hedonist ideology, however, makes it more identifiable to the critical observer. By insisting on individuals' wish fulfillment and self-actualization, the hedonist view makes consumption more vulnerable to criticisms, particularly of the kind that comes from another biased perspective with a strong apocalyptic charge. Moralism closely follows hedonism. The two ideologies are like extreme poles between which discourses on consumption oscillate.

While the hedonist view explains consumption in terms of individuals' delight, the moralist angle blames consumption for society's diverse malaises. Everyday discourses frequently accuse consumption as responsible for a multitude of contemporary social problems, from urban violence, unbridled greed, and exacerbated individualism to ecological, family, and mental disorders. Consumption is the ultimate reason behind all these issues, a kind of one-size-fits-all explanation.

The moralist view of consumption penetrates serious expert observations as much as lay and casual opinions. Condemning consumption is the politically correct answer to give. Those that denounce consumerism can claim moral superiority to those that succumb to their hedonistic impulses.

I do not intend to imply the opposite that consumption bears no relation to any social issues. However, I do want to indicate the apocalyptic character of moralist interpretations of consumption and how these oversimplify the phenomenon as well as the problems that critics connect to it. If consumption explains all things negative in society, then there is little room left for debate.

The moralist bias points to a significant contrast of the capitalist imagination. While consumption is frequently censured and linked to negative meanings, production is usually attached to positive notions. Although both production and consumption generate heated debates, there are significant differences between these two notions when referring to people's practices. To classify someone as a "hard-working," "productive," "committed to their job" (or even as a "workaholic") is to attribute a positive identity to them. Inversely, classifying someone as a "spender" or "consumerist" is to attribute a negative identity to them. That is, production and consumption have different classificatory powers. This difference suggests

4 *Guilt and pleasure*

production and its themes – work, industry, profession – are morally superior to consumption and its themes – brands, purchases, expenses. Production represents what is noble and serious, worthy of respect; consumption, however, is cast as "futile," "shallow," and "frivolous." Like in the ancient fable, the cicada sings, wastes, and consumes, while the ant works, saves, produces. The fable is often interpreted as a compliment to the virtues of work and a cautionary tale against lavishness.

Except for advertising, which is hedonist by definition, media narratives often oscillate between hedonism and moralism. In the moralist mode, they tend to portray consumption as frivolity, craving, addiction, or banality and as morally inferior to production. In particular, the moralist bias dominates journalistic representations. The media makes political, aesthetic, and moral judgments on social facts, and consumption is among its favorite targets. The apocalyptic perspective condemns consumption as a form of alienation or disease, reinforcing production's moral superiority. Production is honorable; consumption is not. Production is a sacrifice that elevates and dignifies humans; consumption is self-indulgence and leads to guilt.

The moralist bias is partly responsible for the difficulties in establishing and solidifying systematic research on consumption. Since the structuring of the social sciences, production was the primary focus of thinkers that wanted to understand and explain modernity. Significantly, the economic axis defines industrial society's singularity. To a central tradition of the social sciences, serious research about society has to think about production and its related issues. Through production, one would be able to access and investigate the political, social, economic, and historical dimensions of reality. The emphasis on production means privileging practical reason, utilitarianism, and evolutionism. Differently, studying consumption means privileging the symbolic, cultural specificity, and the relativity of values.

Biologism is another ideological mark that weakens debates about consumption. The bias of biologism is deterministic and explains consumer practices through "nature" and the "human spirit." The biological perspective combines and confuses the different meanings that surround the term of consumption. This means that a decisive step in the systematic study of consumption is separating what pertains to the cultural phenomenon from the other meanings the word covers.

For example, in expressions such as "the fire consumed the forest," "she was consumed by fear," "they consumed three bags of chips," "his obsession consumed all of his time," consumption refers to biological activities and psychological experiences. Consumption means a natural process of destruction or ingestion and the exhaustion of something's or someone's properties. These meanings are implicitly universalist, deterministic, and individualistic: the fire will always consume forests, each and every life consumes some form of energy. From that perspective, consumption is biologically necessary, organically inscribed, and universally experienced.

Guilt and pleasure 5

But, the dilemma that capitalist societies experience is of a completely different order. There is nothing biological about its brands, fashion styles, car models, soda flavors, department stores, supermarkets, restaurants, banking services, and telecommunications. These things pertain to the symbolic order, where consumption is a collective phenomenon, inseparable from culture. It is to explain that symbolic dimension that a theory of consumption is crucial. It is that dimension that makes consumption an identifiable social experience, culturally determined and historically specific. Confusing this cultural concept of consumption with the other meanings the word might carry is not only wrong but a way of obfuscating the centrality of the phenomenon to understanding modern-contemporary cultures.

To think of consumption as biologically necessary, organically inscribed, and universally experienced is to create a continuum from oxygen intake to the choice of soap as if these processes were the same. Examining consumption through this bias is a political choice that has the purpose of finding a biological and, therefore, deterministic explanation for a phenomenon that belongs to a totally different dimension. Between fires burning and credit card swipes, there is a logical gap. The deterministic bias is to assume a continuity between the first kind of consumption – fuel intake – and the second – differences and choices between daytime and nighttime meals, main courses and desserts, barbecue, sushi, and pasta.

The biologistic view on consumption suggests that a universal nature determines culture. That is, the distortion behind universalist pyramids and other representations of hierarchies of so-called human needs and desires. These representations present consumption as a straightforward progression, from needing oxygen and nutrients to choosing between shampoo brands to fulfilling frivolous desires. By looking for an organic (necessity) or even psychological (desire) explanation for the consumption of products and services, the biologistic perspective hinders investigations of the phenomenon as a cultural system, stripping it of its historical novelty, its social logic, its collective and symbolic dimension.

To understand consumption, one has to avoid deterministic biases concerned with human "nature" and universal biological characteristics. One of anthropology's fundamental contributions is showing that cultures invent and sustain their so-called "basic needs." There is no one common denominator that can account for all experiences.

Closely related to the abovementioned ideological marks, utilitarianism is the last bias I wish to bring into the discussion. The shortest utilitarian explanation for consumption is that people buy things that are either useful or pleasant. In that view, which the anthropological approach long objects to, utility and pleasurableness are inherent aspects of things or strictly subjective perceptions. But, even if moving past these reductionisms, the utilitarian view is predominant in branches of business and marketing studies that focus on consumption as a practical matter of corporate interests. These investigative branches have an applied or instrumental character.

6 *Guilt and pleasure*

Their ultimate attention is on quantifiable results – the increase of sales and revenue. Evidently, these branches' research efforts are crucial for businesses and can bring insights to reflections on the cultural dimension of consumption. However, the notion of usefulness tends to permeate them. The research itself has to be useful, providing instruments that will help improve products and services, boost sales, and generate profits.

The commitment to unveiling the "secrets" to reaching to consumers, to solving immediate and practical business problems, is different from a long-term, broader, and deeper intellectual commitment to understanding consumption. Even if the former can provide clues to the latter, these are two different kinds of hats. The utilitarian bias limits possibilities for building and expanding theoretical debates on consumer cultures because it deviates the focus to elsewhere.

It is worth mentioning that the study of consumption uncommitted to concrete application in the business world can eventually offer very revealing ideas for this same business world. That observation in itself is a broad theme that warrants a more detailed discussion. Here, as an example, I would just like to remind the reader of Freud and his efforts to develop a theory of the unconscious. Freud's motivation to found psychoanalysis was to understand the human mind and open a new perspective on our existence. Indeed, he ended up creating an entire field of knowledge. Through that same gesture, he unintentionally created a significant segment of the health industry. Similarly, on a smaller scale, studies that approach consumption from a cultural perspective reveal ideas that organizations can apply in everyday life. Freud was not concerned with creating a mental health market, but his intellectual drive to understand the human mind and build a theory of the unconscious fomented that possibility.

***

A significant milestone toward the expansion of consumption studies from a cultural perspective was the publication of Mary Douglas and Baron Isherwood's book *The World of Goods: Towards an Anthropology of Consumption* in 1979. The renowned anthropologist and the economist were dissatisfied with how modern economic theory approached consumption as the mere final tip of production and a private experience. Douglas and Isherwood looked to escape determinisms and understand consumption in terms of its cultural and, therefore, collective reality. To them, goods are like ritual accessories that establish and maintain social relations. In that sense, consumption is a collective effort to stabilize, even if temporarily, the flow of meanings and grasp the defining marks of culture.

In the years preceding Douglas and Isherwood's work, there had been other important, but not numerous or necessarily harmonic, efforts to acknowledge and explore consumption's symbolic character and importance in modern-contemporary societies. For instance, French structuralist

Guilt and pleasure 7

perspectives and debates inspired works on consumption, mass media, and fashion from authors such as Jean Baudrillard (1968/2005, 1970/1998) and Roland Barthes (1957, 1964, 1967/1990). In anthropology, Marshall Sahlins (1976) made his significant contribution in an extensive chapter of *Culture and Practical Reason* in which he discusses "*La pensée bourgeoisie.*"

In the 1980s, consumption research had an inspiring moment with contributions from anthropological, sociological, and historical perspectives (Miller, 1981; Williams, 1982; Rocha, 1985; Appadurai, 1986; Campbell, 1987; Miller, 1987; McCracken, 1988). Significant advances have been made ever since, despite the difficulties of defining the concept of consumption and the study topics that concern the theme (Graeber, 2011). More connected to the fields of marketing and business administration, the research current known as consumer culture theory flourished from the confluence of cultural and critical contributions, and has been paving its own path ever since (Arnould & Thompson, 2005, 2018). In anthropology, sustaining an identifiable program has been a bit more challenging (Graeber, 2011), perhaps because consumption blends in different subdisciplines and research branches such as material culture studies, economic anthropology, and business anthropology (Miller, 1987, 2010; Wilk, 1996, 2010; Malefyt & Morais, 2012, 2017).

In my research trajectory, I pick up from Douglas and Isherwood's (1979) work and explore consumption as a system that actualizes culture and is inseparable from it. To me, the anthropological approach is a way of avoiding the biases of hedonism, moralism, biologism, and utilitarianism that constantly threaten to limit and deviate broader studies on consumption.

With *Advertising and Consumption*, I aim to contribute to the study of consumption and its relationship with advertising and media representations in general from a cultural perspective. The chapters that follow are based on different research undertakings I have had over the years but connect through two overarching theories. First, I support the study of consumption as a classification system that materializes culture and creates relations between people and goods, amongst goods themselves, and amongst people themselves. Second, I understand advertising is a mode of magical thought that mediates the passage from the machine-driven sphere of "production" to the humanized sphere of "consumption."[1]

The following chapters are divided into two parts. The first part brings texts that offer perspectives on advertising and capitalist imagination through fieldwork experiences. Chapters 2 and 3 refer to ethnographic research I did in advertising agencies and with consumers in Rio de Janeiro during my graduate studies and in the immediate subsequent years. In "Totemism in the Market," I explore Levi-Strauss's perspective on totemism to propose that advertising is an expression of magical thought in contemporary capitalist societies, operating a classification system that converts the indistinct, impersonal, and serialized outputs of production into meaningful goods available for consumption. In "A Tribe of White Collars,"

8 *Guilt and pleasure*

I expand on that argument by showing ad professionals are like "bricoleurs" who address their creative tasks by reusing and rearranging fragments of knowledge already available to them. "Against Capital" looks back to my experience with the Terena, an original people of Brazil, during the summer of 1985. Based on a theoretical review on interethnic contact and ethnocide, I discuss the Terena's resistance to embrace capitalist thoughts and practices as a way of avoiding assimilation and maintaining their cultural identity.

Essays in the second part discuss female ideals and sports celebrities in consumer culture through the analysis of media representations. In "The Woman in Pieces," I show that, in contrast to the climate of re-democratization and feminist movements of the 1980s in Brazil, the woman in magazine ads of that decade was silent and let products speak on her behalf. "Classified Beauty," coauthored with Marina Frid, investigates female body images in Brazilian women's magazines published in the 2010s, furthering ideas developed in Chapters 2 and 5. Our analysis of stories, advice columns, and ads shows magazines classify an extensive array of goods in relation to female body parts through a logic resembling magical thought. The final chapter, "A Star Player in the World of Goods," coauthored with William Corbo, explores newspaper stories and ads of the 1930s and 1940s to analyze the construction of the celebrity image of soccer player Leônidas da Silva, known as Diamante Negro (Black Diamond). Long before the advent of world-famous players like Pelé, Cristiano Ronaldo, Messi, and Neymar, Leônidas became so popular in Brazil that a chocolate factory even launched a candy bar called *Diamante Negro*, which exists till today, in his honor. We argue that his stardom in the fields and in advertising is a precursor to the current model that articulates sports to a broader consumption system.

Consumption is a signification system; the needs it satisfies are symbolic ones. Like a code, consumption translates cultural categories and relationships between objects, humans, and social groups. In industrial societies, mass media, particularly advertising, have the crucial role of expressing and teaching this code. Through ads and other media representations, products and services symbolically become "necessary," "useful," and "desirable." Advertising interprets production, socializes its outputs for consumption, and presents a classification system that allows us to make sense of goods and connect them to our life experiences.

Note

1 Graeber (2011) warned anthropologists against the separation of society into the two spheres of production and consumption. However, his foremost concern was that this separation seemed to him "to push almost all forms of non-alienated production into the category of consumption" (p. 501). In my work, I acknowledge that production and consumption are two fundamental and interdependent pillars of modern capitalism and explore the distinction between both spheres methodologically to understand advertising.

References

Appadurai, A. (Ed.) (1986). *The Social Life of Things: Commodities in Cultural Perspective*. Cambridge University Press.

Arnould, E. J., & Thompson, C. J. (2005). Consumer culture theory (CCT): Twenty years of research. *Journal of Consumer Research*, 31(4), 868–882, https://doi.org/10.1086/426626.

Arnould, E. J., & Thompson, C. J. (2018). *Consumer Culture Theory*. Sage.

Barthes, R. (1957). *Mythologies*. Éditions du Seuil.

Barthes, R. (1964). Rhétorique de l'image. *Communications*, 4, 40–51.

Barthes, R. (1990). *The Fashion System* (M. Ward, & R. Howard, Trans.). University of California Press. (Original work published 1967).

Baudrillard, J. (1998). *The Consumer Society: Myths and Structures* (C. Turner, Trans.). Sage Publications. https://www.doi.org/10.4135/9781526401502 (Original work published 1970).

Baudrillard, J. (2005). *The System of Objects* (J. Benedict, Trans.). Verso. (Original work published 1968).

Campbell, C. (1987). *The Romantic Ethic and the Spirit of Modern Consumerism*. Basil Blackwell.

Douglas, M., & Isherwood, B. (1979). *The World of Goods: Towards an Anthropology of Consumption*. Basic Books.

Graeber, D. (2011). Consumption. *Current Anthropology*, 52(4), 489–511. https://doi.org/10.1086/660166.

Malefyt, T., & Morais, R. (2012). *Advertising and Anthropology: Ethnographic Practice and Cultural Perspectives*. Bloomsbury.

Malefyt, T., & Morais, R. (2017). *Ethics in the Anthropology of Business: Explorations in Theory, Practice, and Pedagogy*. Routledge.

McCracken, G. (1988). *Culture and Consumption: New Approaches to the Symbolic Character of Consumer Goods and Activities*. Indiana University Press.

Miller, D. (1987). *Material Culture and Mass Consumption*. Wiley-Blackwell.

Miller, D. (2010). *Stuff*. Polity.

Miller, M. (1981). *The Bon Marché: Bourgeois Culture and the Department Store, 1869–1920*. Princeton University Press.

Rocha, E. (1985). *Magia e capitalismo*. Brasiliense.

Sahlins, M. (1976). *Culture and Practical Reason*. The University of Chicago Press.

Wilk, R. (1996). *Economies and Cultures: Foundations of Economic Anthropology*. Westview Press.

Wilk, R. (2010). Consumption embedded in culture and language: Implications for finding sustainability. *Sustainability: Science, Practice and Policy*, 6(2), 38–48. https://doi.org/10.1080/15487733.2010.11908048.

Williams, R. (1982). *Dream Worlds: Mass Consumption in Late Nineteenth Century France*. University of California Press.

Part I

Perspectives on consumption through fieldwork experiences

2 Totemism in the market
Lévi-Strauss as an inspiration for consumption research

1 Capitalism and totemic orderings

This chapter discusses the cultural meanings of consumption, particularly advertising's role in mediating relations between people and goods. I take consumption as a value system at the center of everyday life in Western societies. By investigating this system's meanings, I aim to unveil dimensions of the collective imagination. The study of consumption is a path for understanding beliefs and ideals at play in the cultural order that media representations and shopping experiences actualize. Advertising – namely, narratives and images that have the central goal of promoting brands, products, and services – is consumption's most emphatic form of expression and, for that reason, an almost indispensable pillar for the viability of media enterprises. Hence, the study of advertising has a lot to contribute to the broader project of comprehending modern-contemporary culture.

In my perspective, I avoid arguments that confine reflections about the phenomenon of consumption to the limits of moral, economic, or biological judgments. Consumption has obvious ideological and practical importance in the capitalist world. It is a social fact (Durkheim, 1970) that permeates almost every aspect of social life, structuring relationships, creating symbolic maps, and constructing identities. Here, I propose a theoretical perspective for interpreting the cultural logic of consumption, building upon anthropological teachings, especially Claude Lévi-Strauss's works.

At the turn of the twenty-first century, the registered names of newborns revealed the pervasiveness of consumption and advertising as mechanisms of social distinction and identity-making in American culture. Based on data released by the Social Security Administration, Lopes (2005) found that many brands from the fashion, car, cosmetics, beverage industries, among others, inspired baby names in 2000 – *Armani*, *Chanel*, *Chevy*, *Chivas*, *L'Oréal*. In this extreme consumer experience, humans acquire, through their names, a lasting relationship with brands created by marketing strategies. Thus, a person named *Pepsi* or *ESPN* will, to some extent, have a connection to a market-defined identity. The practice of naming babies after favorite brands is a literal expression of the links consumers

DOI: 10.4324/9781003176794-3

14 *Perspectives on consumption (fieldwork experiences)*

create with products and services, thereby distinguishing themselves from other classes of things and people.

The ideology of consumption provides compelling motives for the production and transformation of subjectivities. "Makeover" reality shows insist that we can and should change our bodies, homes, and habits for the best. Shows like *Extreme Makeover, Extreme Makeover: Home Edition, The Swan, Queer Eye, Fixer Upper, Tidying Up*, and *Revenge Body with Khloé Kardashian* suggest that starting over and accomplishing a better life is possible if only you could perfect your nose, fix your teeth, lose weight, build up muscles, put the right make up on, dress the right outfit, customize your car, repair your house, redecorate, throw away old stuff, learn to cook or garden. In other words, "All makeover programmes are about becoming a better 'you' by making better purchases and adopting better lifestyle" (Banet-Weiser & Portwood-Stacer, 2006, p. 269). An implicit pattern in these shows is the notion of the individual as a set of interlocking pieces that have to fit together according to a predetermined map to function properly in society. Corresponding to these pieces are specific problems that the individual can solve with specialized help – plastic surgeons, physicians, psychologists, personal trainers, hairstylists, makeup artists, architects, decorators, organizers, and all sorts of "experts," which may or may not have a university diploma backing their authority on the subject (Lewis, 2007).

Individuals who embark on these self-actualization journeys want to change themselves to, paradoxically, become "who they really are." They learn to be who they never were in a pedagogical process that aims to make them prettier, tidier, happier, more confident, more agreeable, more prepared for social life (Rocha & Dias, 2005). Their ultimate hope is to go through a genuine "Diderot effect" (Diderot, 1769/2016; McCracken, 1988), meaning new consumer experiences – acquiring new faces, bodies, foods, clothes, furniture, accessories, and so on – will trigger the renewal of all aspects of their lives. These programs attach the individual's perceived unhappiness, discomfort, or unsuccess to specific body parts, actions, and objects that experts can fix or switch. Once the experts "work their magic," the self-actualized participants are ready to be happy because now they correspond to idealized models. Subjectivity itself becomes a sophisticated consumer experience.

Consumption, therefore, should be a central concern in reflections about modern-contemporary societies. Babies named after brands and participants in makeover shows are extreme and clear examples of the phenomenon's comprehensiveness. But the close relationship between culture and consumption is also found in trivial activities like going to the supermarket, using bank services, or dressing up for work (Miller, 1998, 2010; Hyman, 2018; Taylor & Broløs, 2020).

Seminal theories and concepts paved the way to the study of consumption from a cultural perspective. Emulation, gift exchange, ritual, myth,

Totemism in the market 15

classification, symbolic system – these and related ideas were put forth and discussed by authors such as Veblen (1899/2007), Mauss (1925/1990), Barthes (1957), Baudrillard (1968/2005, 1970/1998), Sahlins (1976), Mary Douglas (with Baron Isherwood, 1979), and Bourdieu (1979/1987) and inspired many works that significantly advanced, from the 1980s onward, research on consumption and its devoted pair, advertising.[1] Here, I aim to contribute to this field by presenting my interpretation and use of two works that Lévi-Strauss published in 1962, *Le Totémisme Aujoud'Hui* and *La Pensée Sauvage*. Both these studies are not directly concerned with Western societies or capitalism but offer a solid theoretical perspective for investigating advertising and consumption. In particular, I focus on how Lévi-Strauss demonstrates the so-called totemism is a classification system that articulates differences and similarities between nature and culture, a way of making sense of the world that can exist in any culture.

Two of Lévi-Strauss's most famous quotes are from these books. His line "We can understand, too, that natural species are chosen not because they are 'good to eat' but because they are 'good to think'"[2] in *Le Totémisme Aujoud'Hui* refers to the symbolic character of the so-called natural world and the conversion of meaningless matter into material culture. The other line, "One classifies as best one can, but one classifies,"[3] from a footnote in *La Pensée Sauvage* reveals the human urge to organize living beings and things through oppositions that simultaneously combine and differentiate the available elements.

According to Lévi-Strauss, totemic systems operate codes that translate messages between two parallel series, "nature" and "culture." In fact, totemism intends to overcome the discontinuity between these two series. To give a simplified example, suppose a human community feels compelled to organize itself and its relations with the surrounding elements of nature. The community then subdivides itself into three clans, each corresponding to an animal. Clan A corresponds to the bear, B to the eagle, and C to the turtle. That is, this classification scheme creates alliances between "nature" and "culture." By the same token, the association to these different species of animals establishes differences within the otherwise homogenous group of humans, beings of the same species. So, the correlations between "nature" and "culture" elements simultaneously create distinctions within both series and between pairs (clan A ≠ clan B ≠ clan C). All six elements, however, have complementary relations. Clan A only exists and has meaning if there are clans B and C (DaMatta, 1981).

A crucial insight that Lévi-Strauss had while studying the problem of totemism is that the notion of "nature" is itself relative to each culture. There is no one absolute and universal definition of the "natural" world. Still, in his understanding, the multiple cultural conceptions of "nature" share a common underlying premise: "nature" is the sphere exempt from the human dimension, a sphere that can include anything classified as nonhuman. Nature is the "other." That notion opens a possibility for understanding the

16 *Perspectives on consumption (fieldwork experiences)*

capitalist system as constituted by two fundamental and opposite spheres that mirror the nature/culture binary. Production is the nonhuman sphere, while consumption is the human.

My approach to the investigation of advertising explores the parallelism between the oppositions of nature/culture and production/consumption (Rocha, 1985). In capitalist societies, production is the sphere that alienates humans (Marx, 1867/1977). Advertising is a code that converts "production" into "consumption" in a way similar to totemic systems that convert messages between "nature" and "culture."

Production is meaningless until acquiring a symbolic dimension and a place in the arena of consumption. The outputs of impersonal and automated factories bear no inherent value and need to be invested with meanings to integrate social life. Production only fulfills its purpose once turned into consumption, but to reach its destination, it needs to gain human-like properties. Borrowing the title of Foucault's classic book, *Les Mots et les Choses*, we can say that production is the sphere in which "things" and "words" are in disjunction. Production in itself means nothing; it says nothing. As Sahlins, paraphrasing Marx (1941/2011), recalls, "Without consumption, the object does not complete itself as a product: a house left unoccupied is no house" (Sahlins, 1976, p. 169). There has to be a code to transform lifeless matter into artifacts that have identities, purposes, qualities, places, and relationships in the sphere of consumption.

Consumption articulates and classifies things and people, objects and intentions, goods and identities. In that sphere, products communicate with each other, with consumers, and vice versa. Children's toys, for example, often only make sense as part of "series" or "sets," in certain circumstances, and in relation to specific consumer publics. Clothes "marry" personalities. Furnitures "agree" with each other and "explain" the house. Products and services express desires, feelings, and moments in our lives. That is why the idea that things "go together" is so common. Shoes can match bags, places, desires, moods, states of mind, social positions.

It is my argument that advertising operates the conversion of production to consumption, creating connections within and between series of goods and consumers. To investigate advertising from a cultural standpoint, I turn to the notion of classification, inspired by Lévi-Strauss's approach to the question of totemism. His perspective offers a solid framework to investigate consumption, particularly the language it speaks, advertising.

2 Advertising and classification

The manifest function of advertising is to sell products, create markets, and increase consumption. But is that its sole and exclusive mission? It is conceivable that all the paraphernalia that ads involve – time, people, offices, money, technology – and the ideas they incorporate so emphatically in our social life do more than just sell. To think otherwise is presuming

Totemism in the market 17

that advertising messages have an absolute exactitude, overlooking the existence of polysemy. A closer look at the advertising system challenges the notion that it has an exclusive, well-defined function. People consume more ads than they consume actual goods. The consumption of ads and the consumption of products are separate experiences.[4] Ads go beyond the sale of the advertised product, promoting lifestyles, worldviews, sensations, emotions, relationship models, and social categories in significantly larger portions. Access to products and services is limited to those who can afford them. Ads, however, are available to anyone. Advertising has a lot of room to talk to society and about society. When I interviewed an adman named Alex[5] for this research, he was aware of the fact that advertising does more than sell goods, maintaining a kind of exploratory relationship with social reality:

> Ads are the reflex of a Brazilian moment. I see things that way. I believe advertising is a very strong social symptom. I think perhaps the history of a country, a period, can be told more by ads than by the facts themselves. Because, in ads, there is an entire history that always follows the social in a subjectively defined way. I mean, you can extract these elements and piece up a history, possibly a lot more real, because it is indirect; it necessarily is an account. The subjectivity of all that material can paint, I believe, a much more truthful profile of society.
>
> – Alex

His statement supports the following idea quite eloquently and explicitly. Ads are narratives about our lives, and studying them can point to relevant discussions for grasping collective representations and the very ideology of bourgeois thought. The investigation of advertising can reveal the values, beliefs, and models that guide social practices and how people relate to things and other beings in specific places and moments.

To interpret ads, we must first understand intellectual mechanisms that operate in the process of their creation and within them. Regarding the creative process, one of the mechanisms is the mode of knowledge that informs advertising professionals in their work, which Lévi-Strauss (1962b) identified as "bricolage." Advertising professionals are like bricoleurs whose knowledge mixes bits of different disciplines, theories, and information types. As we will see in Chapter 3, this finding supports an analogy between ads and myths. Both originate through similar logical principles.

Related to bricolage is a logic of classification that operates within ads. The views of research interlocutors were crucial for me to grasp that logic. First, they are the ones who make or consume ads; second, they know the codes of their social world. Interlocutors' perspectives not only contribute with clues for interpretation but help researchers avoid their preconceived ideas. In another work, the analysis of informants' discourse led me to identify a collective narrative surrounding an ad for *Smirnoff* vodka. Moreover,

18 *Perspectives on consumption (fieldwork experiences)*

through that analysis, I understood that elements present in that advertising message built a classification system that differentiated the advertised product from other brands of vodka and types of beverages through establishing corresponding differences between the states of mind, lifestyles, settings, clothes, and habits of different consumer groups within society (Rocha, 1985).

This classification system, characteristic of the "science of the concrete" (Lévi-Strauss, 1962b), fulfills the translation of the sphere of production into the sphere of consumption. The task of relating two spheres – production and consumption – appeared as something fundamental to ads as decoded by interlocutors. By endowing products with names, identities, stories, colors, associations, and positions in the market, ads humanize machine-made, serialized, and anonymous things. In this operation, ads attach objects to elements from the social and the psychological universes, leading the outputs of production toward the human or cultural domain. Ads and the advertising system itself are mediators between production and consumption.

Here, I want to discuss the recurrent presence of animals in ads to demonstrate the workings of this totemic type of classification. Animals play all sorts of characters in commercials and often act as the official mascots or "faces" of brands. Tigers, lions, jaguars, dogs, horses, rabbits, meerkats, pigs, chickens, among other creatures, populate the world of advertising. See, for example, *Budweiser*'s "Lost Dog" commercial for the 2015 *Super Bowl*, *Mercedes-Benz*'s "Chicken" on the magic body control technology, *The Guardian*'s 2012 Cannes Lion winner "Three Little Pigs," the meerkat Aleksandr Orlov of *Compare the Market* campaigns, Tony the Tiger of *Kellogg's Frosted Flakes*, Chester Cheetah of *Frito-Lay's Cheetos*, among many others. I will study the reasons for such regular connections between animals and consumer goods. The advertising system seems to find endless inspiration in the animal kingdom. As totemic operators, anthropomorphic representations of animals are conduits for the human meanings that advertising attributes to products, those elements that come from the nonhuman domain.

The case of animals in advertising is interesting because it also shows an inversion that highlights the modern Western imagination of the categories of "nature" and "culture." In "real" life, animals are part of nature, removed from the sphere of culture.[6] In advertising representations, however, they have human qualities and help integrate elements of the nonhuman sphere of production (nature) into the sphere of consumption (culture), turning them into snacks, beers, comfort technologies, information services, and so on. In the remainder of this chapter, I will analyze how a group of interlocutors explains a selection of ads with animal characters in them. Through this analysis, I hope to demonstrate that by humanizing creatures of "nature," advertising also humanizes products and services, inserting them in networks of social relations, everyday activities, and ritualized experiences.

Totemism in the market 19

In the words of Clifford Geertz (1973), "Culture is public because meaning is" (p. 12). As cultural facts, ads are texts that weave publicly shared meanings (Barber, 2007). There are various possible methods for interpreting these texts. I decided to approach ads with animals through the points of view of people who create and consume them. Hence, my first steps involved determining how to select ads and informants.

Even if a product or service aims at a specific consumer segment, its ads can end up being consumed indistinctly by different groups. Some sectors of society recognize themselves in advertising contents, while others see life aspirations in ads. The diffusion of commercials, be that through print, radio, television, or digital media, is sufficiently broad to make them more accessible than the advertised products and services. Even if published in niche magazines, aired on cable TV channels, or displayed to targeted social media audiences, there is always the chance that the ad will reach more than the imagined consumer public.

Therefore, I started from the premise that the meanings of ads do not belong to one group only, but can be appropriated by various social groups regardless of their concrete conditions for purchase. I interviewed Brazilians who live and work in Rio de Janeiro, but who come from different economic and educational backgrounds, which means they could have different interpretations about the ads. In other words, I talked to a heterogeneous – in terms of occupation, gender, age, income – group of interlocutors, which included two advertising professionals – a copywriter and an art director – a housewife, an insurance broker, a psychologist, a history major, and a concierge. Table 2.1 identifies and gives more details about each one of them. The advertising pros were creative partners at the same agency and became an award-winning team not long after our conversations. I began by interviewing them as experts on the subject of advertising and then talked to the nonexperts.

Table 2.1 Group of research interlocutors

Pseudonym	Age	Occupation	Other information
Alex	30	Art director	Single, worked with Leo
Leo	25	Copywriter	Married, one kid
Lucia	50	Housewife	Rich, married, two kids; her husband is an executive in the financial market
Alberto	30	Insurance broker	Single
Karen	25	Psychologist	Single, worked in a psychiatric hospital
Pedro	22	Concierge	Single, worked in Lucia's building; his father was also a concierge
Julia	19	College student (History)	Single; her parents are famous artists; she worked sporadically on plays and dance spectacles

20   Perspectives on consumption (fieldwork experiences)

I met most interlocutors through professional acquaintances who introduced me to them, except Pedro, whom I approached after interviewing Lucia in her apartment building. Interlocutors from a previous and broader project (Rocha, 1985, 1995) referred me to Alex and Leo. When I first talked to interlocutors to introduce myself and set up our meeting, I asked them to suggest – off the top of their heads – a couple of ads with animals in them. I searched these ads and used them during the interviews. Considering there were some overlaps, a total of seven brands and ten commercials came up in interlocutors' responses. That is not an extensive sample, but enough for the kind of qualitative analysis I set off to do. The animals that the selected ads portrayed were the tiger, the lion, seagulls, horses, and dogs. The products advertised were from different industries – footwear, tobacco, alcohol beverages, accounting services.

Both experts, Alex and Leo, made the interesting remark that analyzing ads for products and services in very competitive segments is better to understand the "strength" of advertising creation. To them, working for clients with many or heavyweight competitors was more "appealing" because "positioning" the product was more creatively challenging:

> I would say it's more appealing to work, to do an advertising job for a product that has competitors, because that makes you position better.
>
> – Alex

> Which direction can I take? Let's see what the other one does. A competitor means more information, though competition can also castrate you a bit, because, if the competitors go that way, you shouldn't go there too. If you want to follow any path, it's ok, but you have a reference.
>
> – Leo

These statements draw attention to two fundamental points. First, they suggest it would be important to work with a highly competitive product category for an in-depth understanding of the advertising universe. Ads for these clients show more clearly the different positions that products occupy, the set of symbols that correspond to those positions, and the social life domains they frame. Second, the statement makes the conversation or intertextuality between ads explicit, underpinning the notion of an advertising system.

Like myths (Lévi-Strauss, 1962b), ads refer to and transform each other. That also explains why products can change in the same advertising setting without loss of meaning. Very similar settings can frame very different products, like clothes, house appliances, perfumes, or foods. The same happy family with a caring mother and a sunny home can frame ads for butter, juice, soda, or laundry detergent. Sometimes various competing brands in a product category dispute the same imaginary

Totemism in the market   21

space – for instance, in Brazil, beaches in the summer are the preferred setting of local beer commercials. Other times, ads for same category products explore radically different settings, like cars portrayed in cities, desert roads, mountains, woods, and so forth. Interconnections, reiterations, inversions are part of the game, justifying the idea of an advertising system.

3 Animals and consumers

What I want to look into now is the role the advertising system plays as a mediator between production and consumption. Advertising recreates products, singularizes and prepares them for social relations different from those of production. In ads, products and services exist amidst the human, symbolic relationships that characterize consumption. The trajectory of products reflects the substantial differences between both spheres.

Production involves raw materials and machines. Its outputs are multiple, indistinct, and serialized. Anonymity and impersonality are the rule. Humans are withdrawn from the process. The industrial revolution's mechanization that transformed the means of production, established an incisive separation between the workers and the results of their work. Factories aim to neutralize all human traces to avoid mistakes and keep standards. Production is, therefore, free from the attributes of its workforce. By suppressing workers' personal qualities, the capitalist production process removes the human dimension of the things it produces. The process does not depend on specific workers, but on machines that anyone with the appropriate training can operate. The absence of "human touch" means no particularization and differentiation. Production prioritizes uniformity, making it hard to determine the worker's particular contribution to its output (Marx, 1867/1977).

Differently, in the sphere of consumption, humanization is the rule. Consumption is where humans and objects meet, where choices, gift exchanges, sales, and purchases happen. In this sphere, people and goods acquire meanings through their relationships. The classification system of consumption creates differences among objects by connecting them to people and vice versa. This reciprocal classification system operates in daily life and expresses a kind of knowledge or worldview that informs the social body. As Sahlins (1976) indicates, at the center of modern capitalism, meant to be a stronghold of "practical reason," there is space for the "science of the concrete" to flourish. But, where exactly?

Advertising is an instance where we can examine a totemic type of classification in operation. Advertising endows goods with meaningful contents, names, values, functions, and relationships in social life. To convert production into consumption, advertising establishes categories and hierarchies, positioning products and services in a cohesive arrangement. One of the primary functions of the totemic operator is naming. To introduce

22 Perspectives on consumption (fieldwork experiences)

a new product means to integrate it into a network of relations with other products, to give it a personality. Alex and Leo comment on that aspect:

> There is the phase of launching the product when the most important thing is showing the product. As of the launch, one way or another, you have created a personality for the product. The subsequent stages are in function of that personality you have created. And then you can reach a very high stage, very advanced, where you don't even put the product's logo [in the ad].
>
> – Alex

> Through human relationships we can explain that (...). When I am introduced to you, my first presentation does not attribute any qualities to my person. In this case, the important thing is me as a physical fact. After that presentation, I have to sell myself through what I am, through what I do, etc.
>
> – Leo

To exist, first, the product needs to be identified. After the launch, the "the product already has its own personality, the product has a characteristic," so ads can show less of its physical aspect. I asked the experts if advertising agencies are responsible for doing all that. They said:

> It starts from a market factor, but that happens solely and exclusively in the agency. It's the profession's reason. It is precisely to say why this product exists, why it should be bought. So, then what? The agency, using market data, gives it a name. Otherwise, it becomes something totally absurd, right? It gets disconnected.
>
> – Leo

> *Coca-Cola*, for example, is a very prudent client, very rigorous on things. It only lets a product have a personality after a long period. We did a support campaign for the guarana soda that was a lot about ambiance. Now the client thinks the product has a personality, after a launch that was done five or six years ago. So, only after five or six years we can take guarana off the brand name.
>
> – Alex

The discussion about introductions, names, ambiance, personalities, and brands sheds light on advertising's role as totemic operator. Naming is first in the order of advertising actions and results. Advertising is like a baptistery where the most disparate types of products, coming out in huge quantities from different origins, hope to obtain an identity seal. In Péninou's (1974, p. 95) words, the move from production to the market is the move from the realism of matter to the symbolism of the person. A key element in advertising's anthropomorphic representations, the brand is itself an analogy with the person.

Totemism in the market 23

While production shuts the human out, consumption restores humanity to products, placing them in the symbolic arrangements of culture. Mediating the transition from one to the other is advertising.

Lévi-Strauss's (1962a, 1962b) crucial contribution was showing that totemism, also known as magical thought, is a classification system that creates differences within the opposite series of "nature" (nonhuman) and "culture" (human) by establishing similarities between "natural" and "cultural" elements. In bourgeois thought, advertising engenders classificatory operations that establish differences within and connections between the opposite series of production (nonhuman) and consumption (human). That helps explain advertising's anthropomorphic or humanized reimagination of animals and other elements defined as natural in modern Western culture. Advertising animals speak, shop, use, and enjoy products. They are the consumers. The "natural" or nonhuman elements in ads are the products. The experts' comments on the selection of ads touch on that inversion. For instance, Leo clearly stated that all ads with animals and other natural elements were really talking about human values and desires:

> I think all these ads have a relationship with the human even if the human does not show. This here has a tremendous relationship with the human because maybe that's the current ideal of human, and some market segment has that kind of ideal. So, you know, the thing is always related to human desires. All of this, you know, in all of them you find human values.

Leo's statement gets to the heart of the role anthropomorphic animals play in advertising. Ad animals are a means to overcome the discontinuity between the human sphere of consumption and the nonhuman sphere of production.

In response to Lévi-Strauss's perspective, Descola (2005/2013) distinguishes three ontologies or modes of identification by which different cultures seek to objectify nature: naturalism, animism, and totemism. I explore Lévi-Strauss's (1962a, 1962b) understanding of totemism as a cognitive form and a mode of categorization, not as a mode of identification (Viveiros de Castro, 2012). Still, Descola's (2005/2013) definitions of naturalism and animism contribute to our discussion here. Naturalism is the predominant mode of Western cosmologies, whereby the nature/culture dualism is ontological, and the relations between both domains are discontinuous and in themselves natural. Nature is universal, while culture is specific and itself a natural phenomenon. Animism inverts the naturalist worldview: it establishes a social continuity between nature and culture through ascribing human characteristics to natural elements (animals, plants, rocks, etc.).

The interesting point here is that advertising representations seem to give expression to an animist mode of identification that Western culture tends to suppress from its everyday reality. Interlocutors' reactions to the

24 Perspectives on consumption (fieldwork experiences)

selection of ads show how they deal with that upside-down world. First, they recognized the animals in the ads as beings of "nature," though some did not act as expected in "normal" or "real" life. Then, they proceeded to interpret the meanings of the animals in the ads in terms of human feelings, qualities, behaviors, purposes. For instance, Alex, one of the ad experts, interpreted the presence of animals in the selected ads as a kind of shorthand for linking emotions to products:

> Since the animal is a living creature, an irrational being, from the moment you use the animal element, it sustains itself. If you put a person... a person has to act, to justify her presence. In this case, if you put a woman here behind this shoe, smiling [it would be] silly... But, it is an animal, so it can be there. Here is the thing: you don't demand a lot of explanation, there's not a reason, because it [the animal] has a different, affective character, it always comes from the emotional.

On the one hand, animals are different from humans, "irrational," therefore need no explaining. On the other hand, animals catalyze emotions, which make them good characters to place in ads next to products. That is why animals "sustain themselves." Their presence is enough to express certain sensations:

> But, there is a relation. The relation here is a strength. (…) Here, there is a relation of softness with the bird. In *Esso*, you link the entire line of fuels with the tiger element, which is a very visual element (…), in the film, they used a real animal and there was the cartoon too, the tiger's caricature, which also created a ludic spirit.
>
> – Leo

> Over here, talking about the cigarette, the title explains: come to the soft side of life. So, the soft side of life within an essentially urban society nowadays is (…) everything you aspire to is non-urban. In this case, it's an animal. Nothing is better to represent that than a natural environment.
>
> – Alex

The experts' comments above reveal terms that define the meanings of animals and the "natural environment" within the ads. They read animals and nature as "strength," "softness," "very visual elements," which convey a "ludic spirit" and "non-urban" aspirations.

These ideas are also present in the testimonies of nonexpert interlocutors. Animals recall nature – "wilderness," "country life," "forests" – and serve as metaphors for various notions such as "freedom," "peace," "tranquility," "durability," "strength," "beauty," "determination," "wealth," and so on.

Pedro reflected, "the bird is there to show freedom, I think, right? In the cigarette ad, I think, [the animal] must be strength, because the tiger

Totemism in the market 25

is strong, so it must be that." Regarding the lion, Alberto said, "I think it means the shoe's durability, like it's a good, resistant shoe." Lucia thought the animals were elements for drawing people's attention to ads:

I really like animals. For example, the tiger is a beautiful animal. It's an animal that has strength, presence. I think, if an animal is pretty like the tiger is, it draws attention to any ad. It's the same with a cat, a beautiful cat. It also draws attention. Any animal that is beautiful, that has presence, I think we look [at the ad] to look at the animal, I mean, "look at that beautiful animal," that makes us focus [on the ad]. You see an animal like the tiger, you think it's beautiful, wonderful. In this other cigarette ad, the bird recalls calmness, like being in a tranquil place. It's associated to peace, tranquility, stability, energy, calmness, and things like that.

As the interlocutors' readings make clear, the animals do not necessarily mean the exact same thing in every ad or for every interpreter. The tiger can be like a "fortress," evoking notions such as strength, resolve, and beauty. Even so, informants' answers present recurrent patterns. Overall, they linked wildcats to ideas such as ferocity, endurance, poise, beauty, and willpower. Differently, birds represented to them freedom, serenity, stability, peace, and calm:

That's what makes you think you're smoking a cigarette... [the ad] shows a bird to give you that feeling of freedom, of you being in a nice place, you know, in peace.

– Julia

Look, if you put a tiger on your tax return statement, I would connect the tiger to ferocity, to resolve, (...) to everything a tiger can represent in a fortress, ok? A strong group.

– Alberto

A few things stand out from interlocutors' comments on the ads. First of all, both experts talked about animal characters as alternatives to persons. In the world of ads, animals are halfway between humans and the outputs of production. Animals require less explaining to be next to the product. Experts felt it was less absurd or "silly" to place animals next to the advertised objects than human figures. But, they also hoped to associate these objects to human sentiments and concepts through relationships with wildcats, birds, dogs, and horses. This explanation that experts give about their choice to use animals in commercials clearly shows that products are elements of the nonhuman sphere (nature) that advertising needs to imbue with meanings and socialize for consumption (culture).

Moreover, nonexperts were able to interpret the connotations of animals next to products in the ads. Their comments were pretty uniform

26 *Perspectives on consumption (fieldwork experiences)*

and consistent with those of the experts. They could decode advertising representations because ads drew from and triggered connections that are part of a body of shared cultural meanings. Nonexperts made sense of the products and services displayed in the ads through associations with the animals or, more precisely, with the emotions, sensations, impressions, or ideas the animals inspired in them. Lucia went straight to the point: "If you talk about a tax return statement only, without the tiger, it's one thing. But, if you show a tiger, a beautiful animal, eye-catching, you're selling more than the tax return statement." By using animals, selected ads brought the nonhuman elements of production closer to the world of consumption, turning anonymous and senseless things into familiar and intelligible goods.

As advertising representations, animals are culture. Ad animals fulfill the role of consumers. This apparent inversion to an animist worldview favors the classificatory process that advertising seeks to effect. Like totemic operators, ad animals connect things coming out of production to the world of consumption. Advertising integrates products and services in culture by attaching products and services to the animals' physical traits (colors, wings, claws, etc.) and the social and psychological attributes they embody in the collective imagination ("free as a bird," "brave like a lion," "loyal like a dog," etc.).

Evidently, advertising representations in general, not just ad animals, perform the classificatory operation that converts production into consumption. Also, when animals are not protagonists but compose a setting, they still contribute to the totemic reconciliation along with the other elements in the advertising representation. Interlocutors' readings of a couple of ads for liquor brands that had animals as supporting elements corroborate both these assertions.

> You know, I think it means an economic factor, I mean consumption, in a way. The impression we naturally have, I'm led to think they own this farm here. Naturally, they have these horses. It's not a casual meeting in the countryside. I believe it presupposes a whole economic level that allows the guy to have a farm, a ranch, anyway, what he seeks in life, you know? It's not a ride on a yacht. It's healthier, that is, life in the open air but refined, from the moment we feel that that is his property.
> – Alberto

> Both these ads are also presenting something of status (...). They have status. So, they can be in the pretty countryside with a wonderful thoroughbred horse. They have a farm and spend their vacations at the farm, and they always have their products with them, which they are drinking here [in the ad]. These people don't look like they live in a place like this. To me, they're spending time.
> – Karen

Totemism in the market 27

According to the experts, ads have a lesson to give. This lesson is expressed, in advertising terms, as seduction, accomplishment, living with peers, living in society, captivating or engaging people. All these messages, according to the experts, are "ways to soften the apparent hardness of the product." In this sense, goods and humans participate in a game in which differences between social relations, states of mind, and economic statuses define differences between products and services and vice versa. In Alex's words:

> What is the lesson here? Living in society and such, living amongst peers, in a way it's saying: dress this cloth and everyone will like you, smoke *Hollywood* and will have a fantastic woman, drink *Campari* and you will live amazing things. Anyway, these messages are ways to soften the apparent hardness of the product.

Values, categories, hierarchies, and relationships that exist in culture translate into products and services suitable for different ages, social groups, situations, places. That is how advertising positions brands in the market. And, in a recurrent feedback loop, advertising representations inform differences in the culture of the moment. As we can read between interlocutors' comments, advertising attributes meanings to products through establishing connections with other familiar objects, beings, circumstances, feelings, and so on. They can recognize themselves or people that belong to other identifiable social groups in the situations the ads portray:

> In this one, the wine has to do with the party atmosphere, the romantic atmosphere. But, it seems like they are not selling the wine itself but selling social status. I mean, it's not that you are going to drink the wine and enjoy the taste of the wine. It's that, by drinking the wine, you'll have two women, you see, you'll be well-dressed, you'll be eating well, you'll be in a restaurant.
>
> – Pedro

> Well, *Campari* is a thing for young people. Young people are now adhering to Campari. You see that the entire group is young, everyone is young, no one looks married.
>
> – Alberto

> This one looks like a dinner with friends or an evening get-together. It's looking more like an evening get-together. For example, we went out on Sunday and had *Château Duvalier* and then ate some pizza. In this one, it looks like it's a dinner thing, an event. She's very chic. It must have been dinner, nighttime, something in the evening by the way she's dressed.
>
> – Lucia

28 Perspectives on consumption (fieldwork experiences)

Connected to the products are rich, attractive, well-dressed, and young people who have social status, charm and attitude, eat well, live adventures, and enjoy their freedom. These people have friends, make new ones, go out on dates, to parties, romantic dinners, and get-togethers. They have a "social life," and the advertised products and services are a part of their lives.

We can then clearly understand the kind of knowledge that advertising eloquently introduces in society. Advertising's mission is to classify products, attaching them to specific activities, utilities, relationships, places, landscapes, atmospheres, sensations, emotions, desires, concepts. The totemic operator looks at society from a certain angle. Advertising sustains the belief in the reality of classifications of objects and people by presenting a particular worldview. Given advertising is a discourse about social life, its images and categorizations ritualize everyday situations and turn them into magical events.

The transformation of social actors' concrete relations into dramas is a ritualization mechanism that advertising uses. Rituals enhance aspects of reality, making some dimensions temporarily more present and influent than others (DaMatta, 1979, p. 60). For instance, a person's finger is part of a biological continuum, individual and bodily. However, the same finger wearing a wedding band represents a form of social relationship. As in this example, the ritual process involves separating and inserting the element in a new context. Ritualization does not reinvent anything but relocates elements to other unhabitual contexts (DaMatta, 1979).

In advertising, this relocation happens at least in two different ways. First of all, ads themselves are displaced objects in the context of the media that distribute them. Ads are scattered between, around, or at the margins of the "real" or "important" content: news, articles, stories, interviews, shows, games, music, series, films, and so forth. The ad interrupts the reading, watching, or listening. It stands out. Often, ads are unexpected and imply a pause.

Second, there is always something out of place in the situations that unfold within ads. The scenes that ads portray involve social beings and relationships, no matter if the characters are humans, anthropomorphic animals, or other humanized creatures. In this social context, the advertised product is a nonhuman element, therefore, displaced. That is, an element from the sphere of production – the advertised object – is relocated to appear in the dramatization of the sphere of consumption – the ad.

This chapter contributes with some ideas toward a greater understanding of the complex world of advertising. In ads, animals are representations, filled with cultural meanings, available for the classificatory operation that converts from production to consumption. Advertising is a kind of totemic operator, a permanent ritual force, a magical discourse that seeks to overcome the discontinuity between production and consumption through associations that create categories and establish differences and similarities among goods and consumers. The systematic study of advertising is crucial to understand the transition from the unknown product to the brand, from the serialized to the unique, from the nonhuman to the human, from the impersonal to the social relations that mark contemporary culture.

Notes

1 See, for example, Campbell (1987), McCracken (1988), Miller (1998), Malefyt and Morais (2012), Milanesio (2013), Trentmann (2016), Malefyt and McCabe (2020).
2 Rodney Needham's translation of Lévi-Strauss's (1962a/2016, p. 84) work.
3 "On classe comme on peut, mais on classe" (Lévi-Strauss, 1962b, p. 285).
4 Through the notion of "daydreaming," Campbell (1987) discusses how people can engage in consumption without purchasing or trying the physical product.
5 I changed interlocutors' names to protect their privacy.
6 Evidently, cultural hierarchies place some animals closer to humans and others further into the "wild." Human-animal relationships are complex and vary even within Western societies. Here, I am referring to the prevalence of a naturalist ontology (Descola, 2005/2013) in Western philosophical and scientific traditions.

References

Banet-Weiser S., & Portwood-Stacer L. (2006). I just want to be me again! Beauty pageants, reality television and post-feminism. *Feminist Theory*, 7(2), 255–272. https://doi.org/10.1177/1464700106064423.
Barber, K. (2007). *The Anthropology of Texts, Persons and Publics*. Cambridge University Press.
Barthes, R. (1957). *Mythologies*. Éditions du Seuil.
Baudrillard, J. (1998). *The Consumer Society: Myths and Structures* (C. Turner, Trans.). Sage Publications. https://www.doi.org/10.4135/9781526401502. (Original work published 1970).
Baudrillard, J. (2005). *The System of Objects* (J. Benedict, Trans.). Verso. (Original work published 1968).
Bourdieu, P. (1987). *Distinction: A Social Critique of the Judgement of Taste* (R. Nice, Trans.). Harvard University Press. (Original work published 1979).
Campbell, C. (1987). *The Romantic Ethic and the Spirit of Modern Consumerism*. Basil Blackwell.
DaMatta, R. (1979). *Carnavais, malandros e heróis*. Zahar.
DaMatta, R. (1981). *Relativizando: Uma introdução à Antropologia Social*. Vozes.
Descola, P. (2013). *Beyond Nature and Culture* (J. Lloyd, Trans.). The University of Chicago Press.
Diderot, D. (2016). Regrets on parting with my old dressing gown (K. Tunstall, & K. Scott, Trans.). *Oxford Art Journal*, 39(2), 175–184. https://doi.org/10.1093/oxartj/kcw015. (Original work published 1769).
Douglas, M., & Isherwood, B. (1979). *The World of Goods: Towards an Anthropology of Consumption*. Basic Books.
Durkheim, E. (1970). *Sociologia e filosofia* (J. M. de Toledo Camargo, Trans.). Companhia Editora Forense.
Geertz, C. (1973). *The Interpretation of Cultures*. Basic Books.

30 Perspectives on consumption (fieldwork experiences)

Hyman, Z. (2018). Mattresses and moneyboxes: Cultural affordances for microfinance in Jordan. *EPIC Proceedings*. https://www.epicpeople.org/intelligences.

Lévi-Strauss, C. (1962a). *Le totémisme aujourd'hui*. PUF.

Lévi-Strauss, C. (1962b). *La pensée sauvage*. Plon.

Lévi-Strauss, C. (2016). *Totemism* (R. Needham, Trans.). Beacon Press. (Original work published 1962).

Lewis, T. (2007). "He needs to face his fears with these five queers!": Queer eye for the straight guy, makeover TV, and the lifestyle expert. *Television & New Media*, 8(4), 285–311. https://doi.org/10.1177/1527476407306639.

Lopes, J. (2005). *Nome de produto, marca de pessoa: Consumo, publicidade e classificação* [Unpublished master's thesis]. Pontifícia Universidade Católica do Rio de Janeiro.

Malefyt, T., & Morais, R. (2012). *Advertising and Anthropology: Ethnographic Practice and Cultural Perspectives*. Bloomsbury.

Malefyt, T., & McCabe, M. (Eds.) (2020). *Women, Consumption and Paradox*. Routledge.

Marx, K. (1977). *The Capital: A Critique of Political Economy* (B. Fowkes, Trans.). Vintage Books. (Original work published 1867).

Marx, K. (2011). *Grundrisse: Manuscritos econômicos de 1857–1858: esboço da crítica da economia política* (M. Duayer, & N. Schneider, Trans.). Boitempo. (Original work published 1941).

Mauss, M. (1990). *The Gift: The Form and Reason for Exchange in Archaic Societies* (W. D. Halls, Trans.). WW Norton. (Original work published 1925).

McCracken, G. (1988). *Culture and Consumption: New Approaches to the Symbolic Character of Consumer Goods and Activities*. Indiana University Press.

Milanesio, N. (2013). *Workers Go Shopping in Argentina: The Rise of Popular Consumer Culture*. University of New Mexico Press.

Miller, D. (1998). *A Theory of Shopping*. Cornell University Press.

Miller, D. (2010). *Stuff*. Polity.

Péninou, G. (1974). *Semiotica de la publicidade*. Gustavo Gili.

Rocha, E. (1985). *Magia e capitalismo: Um estudo antropológico da publicidade*. Brasiliense.

Rocha, E. (1995). *A sociedade do sonho: Comunicação, cultura e consumo*. Mauad.

Rocha, E., & Dias, P. (2005). *Reality shows: Um estudo sobre a produção e a transformação da subjetividade na cultura contemporânea*. CNPq/PUC-Rio.

Sahlins, M. (1976). *Culture and Practical Reason*. The University of Chicago Press.

Taylor, E. B., & Brisløs, A. (2020). Financial technology and the gender gap: Designing and delivering services for women. In: T. Malefyt, & M. McCabe (Eds.), *Women, Consumption and Paradox* (pp. 103–128). Routledge.

Trentmann, F. (2016). *Empire of Things: How We Became a World of Consumers, from the Fifteenth Century to the Twenty-First*. Harper.

Veblen, T. (2007). *The Theory of Leisure Class*. Oxford University Press. (First published 1899).

Viveiros de Castro, E. (2012). *Cosmological Perspectivism in Amazonia and Elsewhere*. Masterclass series 1. HAU Network of Ethnographic Theory.

3 A tribe of white collars
Bricoleurs in the business of advertising

1 External frontiers: a discussion on professional identity

In this chapter, I aim to understand and discuss aspects of the group of professionals that produce advertising messages. These experts' livelihood is to create ads. Hence, they think about advertising as much as they think about their life trajectories. People usually have hypothesis, theories, and knowledge about their professional activities. They turn their practice into a reflexive activity. In an anthropological approach, it is fundamental to listen to the experts dedicated to doing advertising to understand the meanings of that phenomenon.

During my ethnography in an advertising agency in Rio de Janeiro, Brazil, I looked to capture the professionals' point of view and reflections about their jobs, their "know-how," activities, and productions. I wanted to understand how they identified themselves as a group, how they saw society and themselves in it. My goal was to observe and interpret their actions at work and thoughts on their social role.

Ethnography is a form of microscopic investigation (Geertz, 1973). Through an extended period of acquaintance with a group of ad experts in Rio in the 1980s, observing and listening to them on the job, I hoped to contribute to a broader conversation about consumption and the significance of advertising in modern-contemporary societies (Barthes, 1957, 1964; Baudrillard, 1968/2005; Sahlins, 1976; Douglas & Isherwood, 1979). Diverse authors have expanded that conversation since my first fieldwork incursion, including anthropologists who investigated these themes through ethnographies in such places as Japan, Trinidad, India, and the US (Moeran, 1996; Miller, 1997; Mazzarella, 2003; Malefyt & Morais, 2012). Some of the questions that initially guided my immersion into the advertising universe were: Who are ad professionals? What exactly do they do? What do they think they do? How do they work? What is their place in society? How do they position themselves in society? How do they organize themselves as a professional group? How do they create ads? What do they think about their profession?

DOI: 10.4324/9781003176794-4

32   Perspectives on consumption (fieldwork experiences)

In the introduction to *White Collar: The American Middle Classes*, Wright Mills (1951/2002) begins discussing the social classes the book's title refers to by describing professional types comprised in them. Besides doctors, salaried bureaucrats, engineers, managers, and so forth, Wright Mills explicitly mentions ad pros as "absentee salesmen": "In the sales-rooms, which sometimes seem to coincide with the new society as a whole, are the stationary salesgirls in the department store, the mobile salesmen of insurance, the absentee salesmen – ad-men helping others sell from a distance" (1951/2002, p. X).

Ad professionals, therefore, form a group within the "middle layers" (Velho, 1981) of society. The urban middle layers in Rio de Janeiro are an immense and complex social universe, comprising many thousands of people distributed in various occupations with different levels of prestige, status, income, and power. Because of that diversity, "white collars" form a pyramid within the broader social pyramid that has the proletariat at its basis and the owners of the means of production at its apex. Some of the white-collar pyramid's lower strata almost confuse themselves, in terms of income and power, with the proletariat, while the top strata practically reach the apex of society (Wright Mills, 1951/2002).

The "white collars" contain five fundamental "worlds," which Wright Mills (1951/2002) classifies according to types of occupations. The "managerial world" includes all sorts of office managers and their immediate assistants, in business and in government, who have vastly varying levels of power. The "old professions world" includes physicians, engineers, lawyers, teachers, and other new specialties that emerge related to them. The "world of intellectuals" is "the most far-flung and heterogeneous" (Wright Mills, 1951/2002, p. 142), including writers, theorists, critics, poets, novelists, editors, and so on. The "office world" has bookkeepers, typists, and armies of clerks divided into specialized functions and departments. Finally, the pervasive "bazaar world" is the one that most interests this chapter. Among street vendors, sales clerks, retail salespersons, sales representatives, brokers, market researchers, and so on are ad professionals. In the "bazaar world," ad pros are nearer the hierarchy's top, creating "the slogans and images that spur sales from a distance by mass media" (Wright Mills, 1951/2002, p. 164).

Admen and women carefully consider the limits of their professional identity to maintain themselves in the higher strata of the "bazaar world" and the white-collar pyramid. They have to distinguish themselves from other types of salespeople and control the access to their professional identity. Both these aspects will help to understand and situate ad pros in Rio de Janeiro as a white-collar group.

Clarifying the distinction between ad and sales pros helps to hierarchize advertising as more prestigious than other "bazaar world" occupations. As doctors claim protagonism and leadership among health-related careers, so do ad pros seek to differentiate their position from other types of sales

A tribe of white collars   33

jobs. That differentiation, however, is problematic. Ad pros cannot distance themselves radically from the notion of sales nor deny their proximity to salespeople. Their clients must believe that their services will contribute to increasing sales and profits. Advertising as a profession would not exist otherwise. Even if they say that advertising informs, educates, or instructs, ad pros could not convince their clients to hire and spend money with them if the ultimate goal was not to expand sales. Clients do not spend money with ads to educate anyone. They hire advertising agencies with an eye on expanding their consumer market and profits.

For ad pros, it is important to secure a higher position in the hierarchy of the "bazaar world," reinforcing the differences between them and the not so privileged groups of salespeople. Claude Hopkins, an adman who lived, worked, and published books on his craft in the early twentieth century, admitted the closeness between these occupations: "The difference is only in degree. Advertising is multiplied salesmanship" (Hopkins, 1923/2007, p. 19).

Hence, a key concern the ad pros I interviewed had was showing me the differences between their activity and that of sales.[1] When I asked them if ad professionals were similar to other salespeople, the interlocutors pointed out what they perceived as the clear boundaries differentiating their occupation. Their explanations relied on conceptual differences. For instance, they distinguished between selling an "image" and the "physical" product, "personal" and "impersonal" sales, "individual" and "mass" sales:

> While the adman has the responsibility to sell the product's image, the actual salesman, I mean, any type of salesman, physically sells the product.
>
> – Marcus

> There are two types of sale: personal and impersonal. We, admen, make impersonal sales, since we don't have direct contact with people. We never know how many of them we'll reach.
>
> – Paul

> An ad professional sells to a big audience, to the masses. A book salesperson, for example, sells to an individual.
>
> – Edson

Another idea present in the interlocutors' discourse is that ad professionals give elements, the basis, for salespeople to act. That is, salespeople's work would depend on theirs to be more successful:

> The difference is that admen are responsible for creating an image for the product, a [related] knowledge, a concept, an [idea of] appropriateness

34 *Perspectives on consumption (fieldwork experiences)*

that salesmen use as instruments. It'll be easier for salesmen that have good advertising support to place their products than for those that don't have advertising.

– Walter

Some interlocutors did say their activity was that of selling but in a "gigantic" or "multiple" way. All these conceptual differences refer to the position that ad professionals occupy in relation to consumers. The perspective changes a bit once they consider how they "sell" their services or pitch campaigns to clients that will ultimately guarantee the survival of the agency. Interlocutors still avoided using the idea of salesmanship. They preferred to classify themselves as their clients' "consultants." They sell, but in a different or more special way. The testimony below clarifies and furthers that point:

The truth is that we are all salespeople. The ad professional sells advertising. Of course, we are in a bit more sophisticated profession. We have already removed the salesperson title and changed it to advertising consultant. We tried to climb a bit up in the title ranking. Because, at heart, you will sell an ad to the client to make money. Clients will sell their products, and the way they found to do that is through advertising. [Real estate brokers] cannot analyze anything or add anything to their sales because the merchandise they have in their hands limits them. It is all they have. Our merchandise is time and talent. Our capital goes home at six o'clock in the afternoon. Our capital are people. So, when you start to handle intelligence, you have to be more careful even in the way you sell. (...) So, we consider ourselves salespeople. We don't like saying that word, not that it's ugly nor demeaning, no. We create some charm surrounding our profession. But, really, at heart, we are salespeople. (...) So, ad professionals are sales professionals, but they have to be a little bit more concerned, not with the throughput of merchandise off the shelf, pure and simple. They don't have shelves. They are not merchandise. They have to be a bit more careful in their sale. Again, comparing with real estate brokers, when they close the sale, you make the down payment, and that's it. They don't want to know about the buyer. We can't do that. We have to keep this buyer for life. So, we have to follow-up on that sale's results, live as much as possible what the client knows about its business. That is, the business is a bit deeper, a bit more scientific without being mathematical. But, it's scientific. I'd say that's the difference.

– Marcus

In Marcus's words, ad professionals seek to "climb a bit up in the title ranking" and "create some charm surrounding" their occupation. They do

A tribe of white collars 35

not sell physical merchandise "off the shelf" but "intelligence," "talent," "time," "people." They do a "deeper" and "more scientific" type of sale.

These categories create clear boundaries between ad professionals and salespeople, placing advertising in a higher position in the hierarchy of occupations related to sales. On the one hand, the construction of the group's external limits seeks to distinguish it from salespeople. On the other, these same limits separate admen and women from other professionals related to the field of communication that could be mistaken for them to some extent.

Advertising yearbooks published the addresses of all the agencies in major Brazilian cities. In them, one could also find the contact details of contractors that deliver services to agencies. These contractors provide audiovisual, industrial design, photography, artistic, graphic, promotional, labeling, translation, and many other types of services, including buffets, trademark and patent registrations, event organization, and modeling. Media in general are heavily dependent on advertising revenues. Newspapers, magazines, radio stations, television, cinema, digital media, and so on have a close relationship with ad agencies or at least with the logic of the advertising universe. In agencies, employees hired specifically to keep relationships with the vehicles that propagate ads are usually called the "media" staff. They buy media space according to the campaign strategy that the agency plans and the client signs off. There are also all sorts of outdoor media, some of which only exist for the purposes of advertising.

Everything that makes up the list above is part of a vast network that connects, in varying degrees, to the advertising market. The ad professionals I talked to sought to establish the limits of their identity in relation to other agents of this broader "world of communication" as they did in the case of salespeople. They wanted to define themselves as a group, delimiting a space of their own:

RESEARCHER (ME): Are there differences between the many professionals involved in the world of advertising? In your opinion, who really is an ad professional?
JORGE: See, now, the interesting thing is that Mr. X was elected, is elected the adman of the year. It's not that I disagree with that nomination or election, but I think that he is not an adman. He is a magazine editor – a tremendous editor. A man that knows everything there is about magazines, publishing, I mean, everything about his sector. But he was elected adman of the year. You see, men who work in media call themselves admen. To me, admen are those who work in advertising agencies. So, I define the ad professional as someone who works in an advertising agency! Some say that even those that sell medications are admen. Sometimes people ask me, "Oh! You work in lab stuff?". Man,

36 *Perspectives on consumption (fieldwork experiences)*

that makes me so mad! (...) The adman is someone who works in an advertising agency, in departments connected directly to the client, like creative, production, accounts, media. These are the ad professionals to me. Because there is the secretary, and in her documents, it's probably [written] adwoman. To the union, she's an ad professional. To me, she's not an adwoman.

RESEARCHER: In your understanding, can that express a consensus among ad professionals?

JORGE: Exactly. I would say yes. That's why there was a call out. It was not a revolt. But, there was some nuisance among ad professionals for X being elected adman of the year. "What? It can't be!" He may be the editor of the year, the communication man of the year but not the adman of the year. I'm against his election as adman of the year. An adman to me is someone who works in an agency or connected to an agency. Sometimes clients' managers that are responsible for advertising are also admen because they command things related to the profession, the day-to-day things.

RESEARCHER: So, explain to me one thing. What about the vehicle's contact?

JORGE: No, the vehicle' contacts are not admen. To me, they are just the vehicle's contact.

RESEARCHER: And, what if, say, the composer of the ten most beautiful jingles was elected adman of the year?

JORGE: No way! No, [the composer] could be elected composer of the year but not the adman of the year, no.

RESEARCHER: So, the people who work in parallel services, like film production, record companies...

JORGE: Again, in my view, no [they are not]. To me, the adman of the year would be someone that worked in an advertising agency.

These statements help us toward framing ad professionals, first as a white-collar segment in Rio de Janeiro, then as a group within the "bazaar world" and the "communication world" that holds specific characteristics. Placed at the intersection of both these worlds, the ad professionals I met asserted their belonging without erasing their singularity, making sure to clearly emphasize the external contours of their group and action space.

This chapter results from a broader project that had as purpose to understand the social group of ad professionals and the meanings of their creative works. Here, I turn to the resources admen and women use to legitimize their practice. From my conversations with them, one of the most interesting points of discussion I found in that regard was their search to build an advertising "knowledge." This "knowledge" not only fixes a socially desirable position for the group, but also reveals a surprising counterpart. In terms of logic, advertising and mythical thought seem to meet.

2 The group from the inside: legitimation, representation, and knowledge

The social expectation over a prestigious profession is that it fulfills specific requirements and that its professionals experience rough trials and high rewards. In the case of artistic professions, for example, references to rigorous training, inspiration, and the many challenges faced before the first big "break" are frequent. In the case of advertising, there are also some expectations that the group reinforces.

Professionals that want to raise the prestige of their field activate legitimation mechanisms for that end, creating an "image" of the group for society. For ad professionals in the 1980s Rio, at least five points made up the basis of that image, namely high salaries and standard of living, the responsibility and socioeconomic function of advertising, the profession's history, formal training in higher education, and, most importantly, the knowledge required to perform the job.

Regarding the first point, mythologies of high salaries surrounded the advertising profession in conversations among students in communication majors in Brazil of the 1980s and the 1990s and even in more recent years. Two aspects of the advertising job market that students frequently idealize have to do with how hard it is to get in – it is a "walled" or "hidden" job market – and the financial compensations its talents get. The reality of these two idealizations is less important than the type of professional necessity behind the creation and perpetuation of such expectations.

When I did my fieldwork, myths of the profession's "sophistication" and the "wealth" it provides had already been circulating for many decades. For instance, in *Confessions of an Advertising Man*, David Ogilvy (1963/2004), an international superstar in advertising, explains the importance of using clients' products by saying that, among other things, his car was a *Rolls-Royce*. In the Brazilian context, Genival Rabelo (1956) also describes how the lifestyle of the *Standard* agency's director in 1953 involved a luxurious home with a pool, an apartment, the latest car model, a chauffeur, race horses, and a lot of expenses. All of this may or may not be true. It may or may not apply to every ad professional. That does not matter. The important thing is that these stories are part of an "image" the group creates of itself to society.

At another level, the profession's image sustains itself on the notion that advertising has a socioeconomic function, social responsibilities, and social relevance. To some of my interlocutors, advertising brings many benefits to the "people" by teaching them "hygiene" and how to "brush their teeth" or giving them "choice opportunity." They emphasized the "human" side of advertising that, in short, "allows you to live better." In that sense, "advertising's participation in Western countries is beneficial, highly beneficial for their economy."

Technical books on advertising also focused on demonstrating the profession's importance. Chapters with titles like "The social responsibility

38   *Perspectives on consumption (fieldwork experiences)*

of advertising" or "Advertising and development" reasserted advertising's relevance to the world we live in as something indispensable to the social body's functioning. The author's vehemence on that respect in the fragment below is exemplary:

> Advertising has been slurred, threatened, vilified, and adulated, but it has also been the driving force of national development. The research and genius of modern advertising substituted the old chorus "secret is the soul of business" with the concept of "advertising is the soul of business," and, at last, the more realistic thematic: advertising sells, educates, and stimulates progress.
>
> (Sant'Anna, 1973, p. 46)

Furthermore, interlocutors also attached advertising's professional image to the need for a college education. Their views on communication schools and majors were not all convergent and somewhat ambiguous.[2] Many interlocutors referred to communication majors negatively, underscoring a series of faults they perceived in these courses. Some of them explicitly stated communication courses did not give helpful training to future ad professionals. To them, communication schools were a "complete mistake":

> I've had opportunities to give talks in colleges and observe the curricula I don't see any pros. I see them as a complete mistake. I think the course is new in universities and was established in a way that doesn't correspond to the country's reality.
>
> – Walter

However, one of the most important ways of changing and elevating the profession's status is through its incorporation into higher education and legitimation through a college degree (Hughes, 1971). Ad professionals acknowledged that despite their strong criticism against communication schools, they recommended and basically only accepted job applicants that studied in them and obtained a bachelor's degree. Even if interlocutors disliked the curricula, communication schools are one of the pillars of the profession's social credibility and, in this sense, completely necessary. One of them said:

> I believe [ad professionals] must have a college education, a higher education degree. Depending on the area they will work in, art director, graphic designer, etc., they must have university training in design or painting in a fine arts school. For example, someone in copywriting must master the language perfectly. So, it's very appropriate for them to have, for instance, a degree in communication.
>
> – Carla

A tribe of white collars 39

The requirement of a university degree to become an advertising professional serves first and foremost as a mechanism of legitimation. Even if ad pros admit that college is unessential for the day-to-day work at the agency, they still talk about it as a prerequisite for better professional performance. In this ambiguity lies the nature of the higher education degree as a form of legitimation. This is how one of my interlocutors put it:

> A higher education degree is not necessary. No, it's not necessary for day-to-day work, no. But, as I discussed with a guy here at the agency, I think it is necessary, once you learned the technique, the day-to-day, I think university education gives you a much better foundation for you to know how to handle things, that is, it gives you an openness. No matter how bad your university education is, you already have a basis to think, to know how to think. So, I think that's the least that you can have so later you know how to transform that for yourself. (…) When you don't have a university education, you get trapped in a specific path. I'm not saying that the degree has to be in communication. I think that an excellent economist can even be a good contact, knowing the market, products, sales. I always think of a broader knowledge in any area, in media, in creative, because most guys who work in media, they know only that and don't have a general view of the entire advertising system.
>
> – Milton

As the statement above implies, the relevance of a college education lies less on its direct applicability to everyday practice than on the legitimacy or credibility it provides to advertising professionals. According to my interlocutor, every occupation would benefit if all its professionals had a higher education degree. To make beautiful sculptures, sculptors do not need to go to college, but it would be helpful if they understood the "entire" art system. In other words, higher education is not imperative to "make" advertising, except as a form of legitimation. Hence the ambiguous views that the interlocutors expressed about communication schools.

Another legitimation mechanism that constitutes the image of the adman or woman is the profession's history. An occupation does not understand itself historically because it is old. It becomes a historical profession because it possesses or constructs an identity, a repertoire of legendary events, epic facts, origin myths, founders, innovators, and pioneers that delimits and claims a space within society. Advertising seeks to compose a kind of "heroic genealogy" for itself (Hughes, 1971). The most recommended advertising handbooks in the early 1980s usually had an opening chapter about "the history of advertising." One of them talked about advertising in Ancient Greece, the Roman Forum, and China and the symbols of commercial houses in sixteenth-century England, like the wig for barbershops and the ox head for butchers (Malanga, 1976, p. 18). This same handbook even

40 Perspectives on consumption (fieldwork experiences)

referred to a papyrus kept in the Museum of London that recorded a slave's escape in the year 1000 B.C. as the first ad ever written in the "history of civilization" and its anonymous author as the "world's first copywriter." This very particular reading and appropriation of history is yet another legitimation mechanism.

In social interactions, or at the level of the construction and establishment of a solid representation in society, professionals seek to "dramatize" the tolls of their work to make it the expression of something highly complex. It is as if professionals could impress any audience by translating everyday aspects of their work into a kind of dramatic performance.

For instance, the language that physicians use on patients' bedside often includes a vast range of terms unfamiliar to nonmedical participants in the conversation. Sometimes they could replace these technical terms with others used by nonspecialists in everyday life, but choose not to because of the need to express the exclusivity of medical knowledge that only certified professionals master. Lawyers and judges are also skilled at a very specialized vocabulary practically non-accessible to untrained ears that establishes their authority.

By that, I do not mean the dramatized knowledge does not exist. Behind these professions are extensive and consistent bodies of medical and legal knowledge. What I want is to draw attention to the dramatic performance of knowledge as a form of consolidating the legitimacy and prestige of professions.

When entering an advertising agency, one will quickly notice the existence of a technical terminology and the distribution of activities among staff members according to their differences in function. Technical jargon that only ad professionals can understand is also part of the dramatization of their occupation: "brainstorming," "account," "creative brief," "mock-up," "layout," "jingle," "spot," "directmarketing," "insertion," "banner," "geotargeting," "AdWords," and so on.

The use of technical language gives professionals the possibility to dramatize their work in the presence of third parties. A graphic designer at the agency told me his usual tasks were actually quite simple for someone like him, who mastered a set of techniques. However, if he wanted to, he could make his job seem a lot more complicated for nonexpert observers.

Ad professionals constantly use expressive mechanisms to dramatize their work. Comments about how hard it was to get the first internship (usually unpaid) and for rookies to learn the ropes of the business were frequent during my fieldwork. These representations give prestige to those who pass through all these stages and make it in advertising. Stories of difficult beginnings as interns are part of the mythology that valorizes ad professionals:

> [Regarding] training, usually, every adman begins as an intern. He gets internships in ad agencies and, if he is good on the job, his work stands out, and he is hired and develops his career. I'd say that most schools,

A tribe of white collars 41

I'd say all communication schools are very precarious and nothing like the practice. You get training, if you are lucky (and you need a lot of luck!), at the agency where you get an internship. The intern is, generally speaking, marginalized inside the ad agency. He has to be very good to stand out and continue there.

– Jorge

As the statement above suggests, the internship is a special phase in the professional trajectory. The idea of interns being "marginalized inside the ad agency" denotes they are in a different condition. They are in a liminal situation, in-between the outer world of students and nonexperts and the inner circle of advertising. Interns receive training to complete the passage and become ad professionals. In that sense, internships are like initiation rites through which apprentices acquire the necessary knowledge to perform and sustain a professional "façade" (Goffman, 1959). Their mastery of the adman façade is a precondition for their acceptance.

Hence, the internship is the moment to learn the professional representation and has a very different meaning from the formal, academic learning related to the profession. More than study, the intern has to "live the role" of adman to experience its diverse dimensions. In the words of interlocutors, they have to "practice the profession":

The best school, I think, is the agency itself. Good ad agencies have the obligation to offer internships for these students. Here we have five or six, and I make a point of saying to them the following: we don't have time to dedicate to you. You arrive here, I introduce you to everyone, and then the rest is up to you. (...) Nobody will have time to teach lessons, so you learn by practicing. (...) These two girls that just left at least came to my office to thank me tremendously for the opportunity that we gave them with this internship, you know.

– Milton

Interlocutors identify the acquisition of "practical" knowledge as one of the fundamental conditions for professional engagement. According to Goffman (1959), the idea of "practice" or "movement" is one of the most crucial factors for a social actor's performance. The actor performs a set of "practices," characterized by a preestablished action pattern, for a specific audience. Internships are a way for beginners to practice and acquire the appropriate "façade" to act as advertising professionals.

Among the components of that "façade" and professional "role" is the notion of "advertising knowledge." To play the part, ad professionals manipulate a specific kind of expertise. That is the most fundamental legitimizing mechanism of the advertising world. The analysis of the logic of that expertise brings profound consequences for the understanding of the meanings of advertising images.

42   *Perspectives on consumption (fieldwork experiences)*

3 Advertising as bricolage: between science and art

The legitimation mechanism of "advertising knowledge" operates through incorporating information from other areas of expertise available in society. During fieldwork, two notions came up constantly in interlocutors' discourse, connecting the profession to two different types of knowledge that enjoy a fair amount of social prestige. To them, advertising knowledge is a kind of "science" on the one hand and a form of "art" on the other:

> Admen have, or at least they should have, scientific knowledge of things. The work of advertising as an activity connected to the final product, which is the diffusion of practical information to the consumer, can be compared to that of artists because their activity also requires a great dose of creativity, innovative spirit, and active imagination.
>
> – Jorge

This attempt to appropriate two modes of knowledge of such influence has to do, from the interlocutors' point of view, with the diversity of work areas within an agency. The connection of advertising with art and science results from the task division within the agency. For example, the heads of "creative" departments are called "creative directors," and their staffs include "art directors" and "copywriters." However, professionals of "media" departments deal with "research" and "statistics." In the words of the interlocutor:

> The creative director has to know about copywriting and have considerable knowledge about art. Generally, in most cases in Brazil, the creative director started as a copywriter, but some of them also came from the art sector. Today, we work a lot with the so-called creative partners: the ad is born from both. The copywriter and the artist or "layout man" work together. Obviously, the artist or the art guy has to know how to draw. He has to know about perspective, typology. (...) For the television and radio guy's training, one of the most crucial things is good taste. If he knows something about theatre, cinema, he'd have an advantage. The media guy, a media professional, ideally, should have a mathematical education, should master well statistics and research. For the head of the research department, being a sociologist or psychologist is an advantage.
>
> – Milton

Task division is the basic argument for ad professionals to appropriate the notions of "art" and "science." Ad agency employees are a group of people that has "scientific" knowledge about what they make and "artistic" skills to express the findings of "studies" and "research." That seems to be the image the outside world should ideally have of them. The requirement of

A tribe of white collars 43

such complex technical and human resources sustains the profession's prestige and articulates with the other legitimizing mechanisms that build the adman's image.

Moreover, the notions of "art" and "science" are so elastic that based on the premise that the agency is absolutely integrated, an interlocutor defined every ad professional as simultaneously scientists and artists:

MARCUS: I'd say that he [the adman] is a scientist-artist. [He] has the lab part, he has to have the lab part, he has to have the creative part, the part that lets imagination spring, flow. He has to be a scientist and an artist.

RESEARCHER (ME): He will be both these things at the same time, or are these different sectors?

MARCUS: No. Like I told you, there are no creative sectors, lab sectors. Everyone does everything. Of course, there are departments, but everyone does everything when it's time to collaborate. Let's say we go to the lab to do research on product X [to see] how it will reach the public, how it will be seen, how it will be faced, anyway, how it will be accepted or not. But, then you go to the freedom [part] of the thing. The lab gives you the basis for you to have the liberty to create. So, as I said, you have to be a scientist and an artist. I define the adman like that.

Here we might ask: what do these notions of "art" and "science" actually mean for them? How much and what kind of knowledge goes into making an ad? How do they construct that knowledge and which materials do they use?

Reading advertising handbooks, I noticed there was a lot of concern in demonstrating the amount of "knowledge" that making ads involve. The handbooks read as if society needed to know how complex every ad is. In *Scientific Advertising*, Hopkins (1923/2007) says:

> The uninformed would be staggered to know the amount of work involved in a single ad. Weeks of work sometimes. The ad seems so simple, and it must be simple to appeal to simple people. But back of that ad may lie reams of data, volumes of information, months of research.
>
> (p. 61)

In an effort to dramatize such hard work, the adman creates the image that ads are the result of "science" and "art."

Other handbooks also explored that image. One referred to psychology, stating that there is "logical and scientific reasons" for audiences' attraction to ads (Malanga, 1976, p. 42). Another argued for the existence of "advertising laws," explaining that "the phenomena inherent to advertising present constant uniform relations whenever certain conditions are fulfilled" (Sant'Anna, 1973, p. 48).

44   *Perspectives on consumption (fieldwork experiences)*

The adoption of terminologies and ideas derived from the humanities and social sciences also reflects the effort to transform the making of ads into "scientific knowledge." As in the handbooks, my interlocutors likened their type of knowledge to those of psychologists and sociologists. These were the two fields of expertise they mentioned the most. For instance, on the relationship between advertising and psychology, one of them said:

> Psychology, obviously, because [the ad professional] tickles other people's brains. [Ad professionals] have to know, interpret, feel the response to its messages. I'd say they have to be not a psychologist, but they have to know something of psychology.
>
> – Carla

Another one talked about the relationship between advertising and sociology:

> Admen are dealing with people and have to identify the type of audience they are talking to. So, they have to have some idea of sociology. They have to capture sociological changes happening in various segments of the population. If they don't notice that, they won't communicate well.
>
> – Anna

Statements also referred to a relationship between advertising and economics:

> The potential adman candidate should be very concerned with what's going on in the country we live in or in countries that have a capitalist economy. They should understand the economy. They should have an education focused, above all, on that aspect. They should also have a very good notion of psychology and sociology.
>
> – Paul

Interlocutors connected advertising to psychology because they thought ads "get into people's heads," "tickle people's brains," capture the "consumer's mind." They connected advertising to sociology because they believed ads speak to the "masses," must reflect the "audience's nuances," and grasp "sociological changes" in segments of the population.

But that is not all. Interlocutors also linked advertising to the art world. One of them said:

> All artistic activities, because advertising is a combination of various arts. For example, copywriting is an art. Painting, cinema, a series of [artistic] activities, some directly, others indirectly, are connected to advertising.
>
> – Edson

A tribe of white collars 45

Advertising incorporates knowledge not just from "artistic activities," psychology, sociology, and economics, but from many other areas. The adman always needs to know more. They make ads based on their "knowledge of the human nature," of people's "reactions, instincts, and feelings" (Sant'Anna, 1973, p. 46). In other words, ad professionals are supposed to have a tremendously wide-ranging kind of knowledge. According to a handbook, the "science of advertising" investigates "physical," "physiological," "economic," and "psychological" phenomena. To my research interlocutors and handbooks, advertising borrows something from almost any other field of expertise available and well established in society: literature, sociology, design, physics, psychology, drama, statistics, cinema, mathematics, economics, physiology, visual arts. These fields compose the "science" and the "art" of advertising.

It is hard to think of other occupations that require professionals to master so many perspectives. These different fields make up a large part of the body of modern Western knowledge. It does not make sense for an occupation to aspire to grasp all that expertise. It is a lot to expect from its professionals. If that aspiration were a fact, no one would be able to work in advertising. To make advertising, one cannot have an in-depth understanding of all branches of thought and practice. The adman's knowledge is composed, at best, of bits and pieces of these various fields, which appear in ads only residually.

My interlocutors at the agency were aware of the impossibility of fully mastering all that knowledge. Hence the notion of "general" knowledge was pretty recurrent in their self-definition. They did not think a profound understanding of any particular subject area was necessary, but that having "some knowledge," a "vague notion," a slight "familiarity," "versatility," "eclecticism," or "a bit of everything" was. They do not regard themselves as specialists but as "generalists." Their "general culture" means they borrow from elements from various fields without having in-depth knowledge in any of them. In the words of interlocutors:

> [The ad professional] is a dreamer, an intellectual, a father, a brother, a mother. Anyway, he has to be a specialist in general ideas for his work to have total reach.
>
> – Oscar

> The adman has to be versatile.
>
> – Marcus

> But, I think who works in advertising has to have general knowledge. They do not need to have any profound knowledge but know a little bit of everything – the more the better.
>
> – Anna

46   Perspectives on consumption (fieldwork experiences)

The adman knows a little bit of everything and nothing about anything specific. [They] know about a lot of things and are not specialists. The adman is far from being a specialist.

– Carla

These definitions demonstrate one of the most significant characteristics of the profession. Admen and women manipulate discourses derived from diverse domains of knowledge, but does not delve into any of them. Their specialty is diversity and their knowledge, encyclopedic. They are "eclectic" – significantly, the first ad agency in Brazil was called *Eclectic*. Theirs is a world of "general ideas."

Ad professionals define their field of expertise as made of bits of a dozen others, dispersed, of a generalist kind. The logic of that kaleidoscopic knowledge is to combine every available fragment of information to make advertising instruments.

It is that characteristic that leads me to liken advertising to bricolage. From an inside perspective, the intellectual movement of advertising before a given task is to address it by gathering and making combinations with all elements within reach. For example, creating an ad leads the adman to take a retrospective step. They consult the diverse fragments of knowledge in their toolbox and conceive their plan based on little bits of literature, psychology, statistics, cinema, and so on.

In contemporary capitalist societies, few intellectual activities mirror the notion of "bricolage" (Lévi-Strauss, 1962/1966) as precisely as advertising does. Ad professionals are "bricoleurs" par excellence. They build their knowledge through incorporating elements already available in their social world, having as an implicit principle that everything is usable. Like "bricoleurs," they work with what they have at hand. The knowledge they use to make their instruments is accessible in their social world. This knowledge, however, by the very state of its development, limits the arrangements of instruments they make and use in the creation of their various ads.

A fragment of a psychological theory, a piece of a sociological idea, an allusion to a physical theory, a school of painting's characteristic trace or brushstroke, a literary movement's style, excerpts from novels, references to films, a random account of a personal experience, sprinkles of statistics, and so on are part of a set of components ready for the adman to pick up and arrange in multiple combinations when creating ads. The bricoleur – or the ad professional – can use anything to create, from bits of different kinds of knowledge to a compilation of stereotypes related to consumer publics or the vogue of the day:

His universe of instruments is closed and the rules of his game are always to make do with 'whatever is at hand', that is to say with a set of tools and materials which is always finite and is also heterogeneous because what it contains bears no relation to the current project, or indeed to any particular project, but is the contingent result of all the occasions there have been to renew or enrich the stock or to maintain it with the remains of previous constructions or destructions.

(Lévi-Strauss, 1962/1966, p. 17)

The bricoleur's and the adman's thought do not aim at any particular project. Their characteristic is to amalgamate fragments and scraps, reusing them at the first opportunity. In advertising, as in bricolage, there is no direct relationship between the project and the instruments made to address it. The profession's everyday life is marked by a tremendous variety of projects. That variety is one of advertising's distinguishing marks, and its magnitude inevitably prevents the development of a new set of tools for each project. Therefore, ad professionals tend to make sets – diversified, generalizing, and residual ads – that they can reach out to in all possible projects.

The analysis of ad professionals' descriptions of their own mode of thinking on the job strengthens the analogy between advertising production and the logic of "bricolage." One of my interlocutors tried to explain to me how were his workdays and how his profession trained his way of being and thinking:

> Their (ad professional's) mind has to be alert to everything – everything and everyone. [Their mind] has to be quick, has to be organized. To be able to pay attention to you, pick up the phone, talk to X, say "good evening" to Y, read a telex, smoke a cigarette, etc., I need to have a mental organization. My thinking has to be fast. That's the beauty of the profession. I'm not lessening yours. You are a teacher. Every day, you teach your class. Though you create your little lectures, add a little something new, meet new students that make you different questions, it's always the same thing. It's the same for lawyers, for doctors. Today, we discuss gasoline, edibles in the afternoon, bras the next day. Notice the variety of things you handle. It doesn't tire you. The adman never tires because that's the fun of the profession. Today, you talk about beer, how the beer market operates, distributes, how the consumer thinks, how we can influence the consumer to drink more beer. Tomorrow, you talk about cigarettes, then about computers. You know, you have to have global knowledge, a variety of thoughts, and different strategies. So, there's no monotony. No day is the same. Every day, there's a new fact, a new element, a new debate, a new type of message to cite, a new challenge. You have to read a lot about everything, preferably be up to date on everything.

> – Oscar

The perspectives of classic advertising handbooks resonate in many ways with the interlocutors' views. Regarding the creative process, Ogilvy

48 *Perspectives on consumption (fieldwork experiences)*

(1963/2004) talks about the need to "escape the tyranny of reason" in order to unblock imagination and have "original thoughts." The adman argues that creativity requires experimenting with ideas and following intuitive feelings that spring from the unconscious. Because he was, in his words, "incapable of logical thought," he developed a technique to access the "messy repository" of his mind that involved leisurely activities such as riding a bike, bird-watching, gardening, taking long baths, and listening to music. While he was "busy doing nothing," the adman received the flow of ideas from his unconscious that served as raw material for making his ads. Though Ogilvy speaks of leisure and relaxation, he is still describing a process, which requires discipline, hard work, and "uncontrollable curiosity."

Young (1940/2003) compares the creative process in advertising to the act of rotating a kaleidoscope that forms multiple geometrical models through combinations of the same tiny pieces of glass contained in it. Every rotation rearranges the shards into new and incredible shapes. The more pieces of glass inside the kaleidoscope, the more combinations one gets. To Young (1940/2003), making an ad is like forming a new kaleidoscopic model. Ideas for campaigns spring from combinations between the knowledge about specific products and ad professionals that have general knowledge about facts of life. The more elements ad pros have accumulated in their minds, the more creative possibilities they possess.

A third handbook argues creatives are by definition anti-specialists. They are able to make connections and find relationships between vastly different things precisely because they do not follow "linear parameters" of reasoning nor limit themselves to "homogeneous fields" of knowledge (Barreto, 1978, p. 27).

Interlocutors and handbooks seek to explain a form of intellectual operation typical of advertising work. They describe the making of ads in terms of nonspecialization, connections between different things and combinations of various elements at the creative's disposal, in their mind's repository and surrounding social universe. Advertising's sources of ideas are, at once, miscellaneous and limited to the set of existing materials. In that respect, the adman's and the bricoleur's rationality and modus operandi are the same:

> Consider him at work and excited by his project. His first practical step is retrospective. He has to turn back to an already existent set made up of tools and materials, to consider or reconsider what it contains and, finally and above all, to engage in a sort of dialogue with it and, before choosing between them, to index the possible answers which the whole set can offer to his problem.
>
> (Lévi-Strauss, 1962/1966, p. 18)

A *tribe of white collars* 49

When the bricoleur – or the adman – has a task to perform, their process is to "turn back," reexamine the existing set of elements, and rearrange it in such a way that fulfills that task. Different from the "engineer's" logic, which is to develop specific instruments to address evermore specialized projects, always seeking to go beyond the constraints of their existing toolbox, the bricoleur engages in a conversation with the available collection to extract from it the elements they need to complete their project (Lévi-Strauss, 1962/1966).

Ad professionals consult their mind's "messy repository," their feelings and experiences, their baggage of "general culture." They "pick up" vestiges of stories, images, concepts, and techniques and create connections between them. These assorted vestiges are the raw material of the advertising kaleidoscope. Every time ad professionals address a client's new demand, they reorder the tiny "pieces of glass" – fragments of dozens of theories, representations of social life, personal and collective experiences– to create a new "model" – an ad. The final result of advertising creation materializes a great work of bricolage. In fact, Lévi-Strauss (1962/1966, p. 36) himself also uses the kaleidoscope metaphor to explain the bricoleur's logic.

If the analogy between advertising and bricolage is correct, we have grounds to explore some implications of advertising's presence in contemporary capitalist societies. The bricoleur's logic, which is the intellectual operation proper of advertising thought, is characteristic of other domains as well. In fact, according Lévi-Strauss (1962/1966), bricolage is the mark of mythical thought:

> The characteristic feature of mythical thought is that it expresses itself by means of a heterogeneous repertoire which, even if extensive, is nevertheless limited. It has to use this repertoire, however, whatever the task in hand because it has nothing else at its disposal. Mythical thought is therefore a kind of intellectual 'bricolage' – which explains the relation which can be perceived between the two.
>
> (Lévi-Strauss, 1962/1966, p. 17)

Mythical thought feeds itself of a repertoire that is broad and diversified, albeit preestablished. As a form of bricolage, mythical thought restricts its possibilities to the inventory of elements contained in the society that engenders it. In this sense, there is a logical proximity between mythical thought and advertising. Both have bricolage as their mode of intellectual operation. An ad is a story, a representation, an ideal model of experience. Ads express an ideology built of little everyday facts that connect a product to a way of "good living," to situations and human relationships, to prestige and social status. Ads activate mythical scenes of life improvement through consumption.

50 *Perspectives on consumption (fieldwork experiences)*

Based on their common bricoleur logic, I take that ads can be understood as myths – collective narratives that circulate in society – or as rituals – experimentation and sensible discourse of that society. As myths, ads legitimize power, maintain the state of things, and socialize individuals in a preestablished order. As rituals, ads are society speaking about itself and defining itself.

Among other things, advertising is a privileged space for the expression and persistence of mythical thought in contemporary societies. By that, I do not mean that ads' mythological character justifies its existence. Advertising emerges as a mechanism that the capitalist system uses and supports for its benefit and preservation. However, its interpretation from a strict economic point of view misses the cultural aspects of the phenomenon. Advertising's efficacy lies in the fact that by idealizing life always in the same direction, it becomes the mirror for a social project. Its constant and pervasive presence in daily life suggests it fulfills a "necessary" role and that its images are a kind of second "nature" to reality. In that, advertising also reflects an ideology of everyday life that wants to imprint a sense of stability and "naturalness" in the order of things. Ads conceal certain aspects of reality and direct attention to the specific elements they spotlight. As mediators, ads reconcile opposite levels of capitalism, representing its ideological model free from its deepest contradictions.

Lévi-Strauss (1962/1966) shows that the reconciliation of opposites is a classificatory device of the so-called "totemism." Totemic systems translate messages between the separate realms of "culture" and "nature"; that is, between the sphere that encompasses humans and their relationships and the sphere that contains the other creatures and things – the nonhumans. Lévi-Strauss (1962/1966) understands totemism as a conceptual system that aims to transcend the opposition between these two metaphorical and discontinuous realms that organize social experience.

Advertising in capitalist societies is one of the systems that allow the mediation between different realms. Through advertising's classificatory operation, mass produced, interchangeable, and impersonal objects become unique, personal, custom-made for each consumer. That is, advertising reconciles a structural opposition at the center of capitalism between the realms of production and consumption.

In the capitalist world, production is the sphere of machines, raw materials, and numbers, of human absence and indistinguishable objects. The advertising system converts the lifeless items that come out of production into "useful," "fun," "pleasant," "comforting," "fancy," "luxurious," "exclusive," or even "magical" goods available for consumption, the sphere of human relationships.

Advertising representations create correspondences between familiar and shared values, images, and experiences and the yet unknown outputs of production, glossing over the social history of the manufacturing process and giving new origin stories to objects. In ads, products come to life,

A *tribe of white collars* 51

acquiring names, personalities, feelings, intentions. They become a part of impeccable homes, happy reunions, romantic encounters, thrilling adventures, relaxing moments, and so many other idealized scenarios ingrained in the imagination. Nothing is broken or displaced in ads. Everything has a time and place. Everything makes sense.

By conceiving these coherent and flawless scenarios, the bricoleurs of advertising seek to integrate products into society in a seamless way, as if the objects had always meant to be there. Ad professionals explore their collection of elements, selecting and rearranging them according to the current product. They translate production into consumption through reordering elements and finding new combinations. Their creative possibilities, however, are always "pre-constrained." Like in mythical thought, advertising creativity is only boundless within the extent of the set of elements that exist in social life and are within its reach.

Notes

1 I changed the names of all interlocutors to protect their privacy.
2 In the Brazilian higher education system, advertising is generally a specialty of communication schools and majors since these emerged in the mid-twentieth century.

References

Barreto, R. M. (1978). *Criatividade em propaganda*. Documentário.
Barthes, R. (1957). *Mythologies*. Éditions du Seuil.
Barthes, R. (1964). Rhétorique de l'image. *Communications*, 4, 40–51.
Baudrillard, J. (2005). *The System of Objects* (J. Benedict, Trans.). Verso. (Original work published 1968).
Douglas, M., & Isherwood, B. (1979). *The World of Goods: Towards an Anthropology of Consumption*. Basic Books.
Geertz, C. (1973). *The Interpretation of Cultures*. Basic Books.
Goffman, E. (1959). *The Presentation of Self in Everyday Life*. Doubleday.
Hopkins, C. (2007). *Scientific Advertising*. Cosimo. (First published 1923).
Hughes, E. (1971). *Sociological Eye*. Aldine-Atherton.
Lévi-Strauss, C. (1966). *The Savage Mind*. Weidenfeld & Nicolson. (Original work published 1962).
Malanga, E. (1976). *Publicidade: uma introdução*. Atlas.
Malefyt, T., & Morais, R. (2012). *Advertising and Anthropology: Ethnographic Practice and Cultural Perspectives*. Bloomsbury.
Mazzarella, W. (2003). *Shoveling Smoke: Advertising and Globalization in Contemporary India*. Duke University Press.
Miller, D. (1997). *Capitalism: An Ethnographic Approach*. Berg.
Moeran, B. (1996). *A Japanese Advertising Agency: An Anthropology of Media and Markets*. The University of Hawaii Press.
Ogilvy, D. (2004). *Confessions of an Advertising Man*. Southbank Publishing. (First published 1963).

52 *Perspectives on consumption (fieldwork experiences)*

Rabelo, G. (1956). *Tempos heróicos da propaganda*. Achiamé.

Sahlins, M. (1976). *Culture and Practical Reason*. The University of Chicago Press.

Sant'Anna, A. (1973). *Teoria, técnica e prática da propaganda*. Pioneira.

Velho, G. (1981). *Individualismo e cultura*. Zahar.

Wright Mills, C. (2002). *White Collar: The American Middle Classes*. Oxford University Press. (First published 1951).

Young, J. W. (2003). *A Technique for Producing Ideas*. McGraw-Hill. (First published 1940).

4 Against capital

The resistance to economic thought among the Terena of central Brazil

1 On the road

All was dust. The sun hiding behind the clouds made us feel inside a greenhouse. It was a hot Saturday in Mato Grosso do Sul, summer of 1985. We wobbled inside the old pickup truck, driving slowly through a straight road that crossed a stream. Sweat pasted clothes and mosquitoes to our skins. Outside were birds, butterflies, and a few mares, small crops of rice, corn, and beans along with banana trees signaling the tropical climate. Barbed wires, cattle, grass, and three skinny barking dogs completed the country scenery.

We had just passed a rusty sign painted with yellow and green stripes that read: "Federal Government. Ministry of Interior. National Indian Foundation. Forbidden Area. Strangers not allowed to access the Indian reservation." Articles of the Brazilian Constitution and the Penal code accompanied the alert. Other than the solemn sign, nothing much distinguished the entrance of the Terena reservation from those of the neighboring farms in the administrative area of the municipality of Nioaque.

A thousand questions popped into my head just from reading that sign. Who can donate lands to people who had already been their inhabitants for centuries? Was I entering a country inside another country? A culture within a culture? Was that Terena or Brazilian territory? Were the people Terena-Brazilian or Brazilian-Terena? Luís Terena traveled next to me, sitting by the car window.[1] When we met a couple of days earlier, he defined himself as a pure Terena, father to pure Terena children and descendant of the many Terena who lived before him and were the first to occupy that land, before other indigenous peoples and way before "whites." To him, the sign came in third place. However, the sign still troubled me, especially in light of Pierre Clastres's (1980/2010, pp. 104–105) comments regarding the Brazilian State policy on original peoples[2]:

> "Our Indians", proclaim the administrators, "are human beings like anyone else, but the savage life they lead in the forests condemns them to poverty and misery. It is our duty to help them emancipate themselves

DOI: 10.4324/9781003176794-5

54 *Perspectives on consumption (fieldwork experiences)*

from servitude. They have the right to raise to the dignity of Brazilian citizens in order to participate fully in the development of the national society and enjoy its benefits." The spirituality of ethnocide is the ethics of humanism.

Thus, the sign translated the paradox between the official government policy and the viewpoint of those who are the object of that policy. While the latter restated their identities as "pure" Amerindians, the former subtracted that identity and in its place established the vague "dignity of Brazilian citizens" who are participants in the (problematic) national development.

Luís Terena's notion that his people were "the first" in that land is characteristically ethnocentric. But, ethnocentrism is a trait that most, if not all, human cultures share (Lévi-Strauss, 1952; Rocha, 1984). Cultures tend to think of themselves as the "center," the "first," the "better," the "human," and so on. "Our" group usually perceives the "others" in a hierarchical sense as a negative difference and vice versa. The Terena have ethnocentric notions, and so do other social groups in Brazil. The sign, however, brought more than the concept of ethnocentrism to mind. By recalling the State policy and more broadly a general attitude toward "Indians," the sign escalated from ethnocentric ideas to an ethnocidal practice.

It is worth pausing here for a brief discussion on the meanings of three words: ethnocentrism, genocide, and ethnocide. Ethnocentrism translates how we often see and experience the world by taking our group – our habits, beliefs, values – as the standard for interpreting and judging everything and everyone. Genocide is a legal concept created in 1946 during the Nuremberg trials (Clastres, 1980/2010, p. 101) that characterizes the practice of systematic extermination of humans from specific races, ethnics, or cultures. The mass killing of Jews by Nazism was the first case tried as a genocide crime. According to its legal definition, genocide is rooted on and results from racism. Ethnocide is a more complex notion.

Unlike the physical extermination that characterizes genocide, ethnocidal practice aims the destruction of a culture. Ethnocide means to systematically eliminate the manners of thought and expression, in fact, the entire manner of existence of subjugated cultures. All cultures are ethnocentric, but only some are ethnocidal. Clastres (1980/2010) indicates that ethnocidal cultures are characteristic of societies with a State and whose regime of economic production does not tolerate the kind of difference expressed by the denial of productivity.

Genocide and ethnocide are distinct practices but can happen together. Zelito Vianna's documentary film *Terra dos Índios* (Brazil, 1979) shows a macabre example of that combination. In a poignant scene, an elder woman, the last living member of her tribal group, dramatically reacts when listening to her voice emanating from the production team's recorder. Her group did not exist anymore. She had not heard or spoken her native language for a long time. Her culture had been destroyed by ethnocidal practices and the

Against capital 55

few surviving members had been separated from each other. By the time of filming, her culture had vanished and she was the only remaining representative. The scene portrays probably the most radical form of solitude that a person can experience. Genocide kills the physical body. Ethnocide kills the spirit.

The contrasts and contradictions materialized by the sign at the entrance of the Terena reservation inspired my reflections about the experiences and exchanges I had with the Terena during that summer. On the one hand, Luís Terena's words had a clear affirmation: the affirmation of cultural identity, the certainty of being Terena. On the other, the Terena had been in contact with Western cultures in Brazil for over 300 years, oscillating between phases of moderate and intense interactions. Since the late nineteenth century, the ever-increasing regularity and asymmetry of their relations with non-indigenous society or the national society meant they were under the permanent threat of an ethnocidal culture. The incredible resistance of being Terena despite the constant attempts of ethnocide intrigued me.

Roberto Cardoso de Oliveira had noted that same strong sense of identity among the Terena of the municipalities of Miranda and Aquidauana in the 1950s. In the preface of his book *O Processo de Assimilação dos Terena* (*The Process of Assimilation of the Terena*), Darcy Ribeiro wrote:

> The theme of this study is the analysis of the explicative potentialities of this rare case in Brazil of a tribe that went practically all the way to acculturation, preserving a ponderable population size that reached a high degree of participation in regional life, but, despite that, remains differentiated, identifying itself and being identified as indigenous.
> (Cardoso de Oliveira, 1976, p. 14)

A people that went down the path of acculturation, as did the Terena, would normally have reached the point of disappearing as a culture. What is impressive about the Terena is the fact that they remained Terena! Cardoso de Oliveira (1976, p. 24) demonstrates his perplexity with the strength of their resistance: "(...) why the Terena, despite centuries of continuous and systematic contact with Brazilian population groups, still remain Indians, even after being integrated within the regional economic structure? What are the mechanisms that have been obstructing the paths to assimilation?"

These questions that for long have occupied anthropologists may still bring new perspectives. This chapter returns to that discussion, showing that what enables the Terena to go through acculturation without losing their identity is the refusal to accept basic parameters of the national society's way of life. In other words, what has been "obstructing the paths to assimilation" is a strategy of being Terena that sustains itself in the denial of Western values represented by "Brazilian population groups." Precisely, I would like to explore the hypothesis that a central aspect of being Terena lies in their resistance against integrating "regional economic structure."

56 *Perspectives on consumption (fieldwork experiences)*

From the perspective of the regional economy, national society has integrated the Terena. But, from their point of view, the Terena exempt themselves from that integration as a way of resisting.

This chapter investigates the question of Terena integration in light of the relationship they maintain with the regional economy. I will discuss that relationship based on Cardoso de Oliveira's data and mine. Through my observations at the villages of Brejão and Pedra Branca and conversations with Terena individuals in the reservation and a neighboring farm, I learned aspects of their cultural imagination and behavior that reveal a particular view on the meanings of things such as "economy," "work," "consumption." Also, I was able to observe up close the behavior of local farmers and hear their ideas about the "land," the "Indians," and the "economy." The evident mismatch between the farmers' and the Terena's view on "productive work" is crucial to explain why the latter continued to see themselves and be seen as Amerindians despite the process of acculturation.

I aim to show how the Terena's way of participating in the regional economy is a strategy to mark their difference. To do so, I will first describe the Terena people, reviewing previous works on them, especially Roberto Cardoso de Oliveira's studies. Then, I will discuss the notions of historicism, productivism, individualism, and the State as pillars of the Western worldview, recounting two experiences I had in the "regional economy" – one with the Terena and another with non-indigenous farmers. I discuss the particularity of each experience and the differences they reveal. Finally, I discuss the question of Terena's "integration" into the "regional economy." My point is to understand their strategy for affirming their cultural identity, either by the systematic denial of the capitalist productivity logic or their refusal to submit their whole life to the economic dimension.

2 From "isolated" to "integrated"

It was hard to distinguish the Terena men that walked by the highway connecting Campo Grande, the state capital, to Nioaque from the other ranch hands of the region. Waiting for a bus by the dirt road, chatting in *bolichos*,[3] herding cattle, or saddling horses, the Terena did not stand out in the eyes of visitors from big cities, usually drawn to elements of the rural landscape unfamiliar to them, such as the strange colors of the sky, the texture of the earth, the vastness of the horizon, large lizards crossing the road, birds flying, and so on. Elements that urbanites associate to the experience of the exotic. It can take visitors a while to understand that among the many ranch hands passing by – wearing plastic boots or flip flops, jeans or shorts, no top or unbuttoned shirts, and straw hats – are men who identify themselves as "Indians" and who other locals identify as such.

The Terena did not distinguish themselves because of how they dressed, talked, ate, or behaved in public. On the surface, they were like everyone else in Nioaque. They had been in contact with "white men" for 300 years.

Against capital   57

Hence, by the 1980s, it looked as if they had assimilated or acculturated. Their difference, however, did not lie in the signs of consumption – soft drinks, cigarettes, gums, beer – that everyone in the region shared. Their difference was not in the habits of drinking Coke or coffee with sugar at the *bolicho*.

Evidently, the difference between "them" and "us" had been much clearer in the past. Their first encounters with the colonizers were through mercenary explorers known as *bandeirantes* in the seventeenth century. The *bandeirantes*' expeditions were instrumental for the Crown of Portugal to expand the territory of its colony. But, these explorers captured and enslaved, if not killed, the Amerindians they met while advancing westward from the region of São Paulo, then called Captaincy of São Vicente. According to chronicles, the relationship between the *bandeirantes* and the Guaná nation, of which the Terena are a subgroup, was violent. Amidst disputes between explorers, Jesuits, the Portuguese, and the Spanish, indigenous groups were divided and used in combats, often fighting against each other. They lost their lands, people, and belongings (Cardoso de Oliveira, 1976).

The Guaná faced the same struggle for survival as other original peoples in the way of Western powers in search of gold, precious gems, and minerals or land to expand their plantations and cattle farms. In the 1760s, the pressure of the Spanish advancing in the territory of the Mbayá, neighbors and allies of the Guaná, forced many of these nations' subgroups, including the Terena, to migrate to the Eastern side of the Paraguay River. This migrant movement probably went on until the early nineteenth century. In 1791, Portugal signed a peace treaty with the Mbayá-Guaicuru, which allowed for the increasing presence of small Portuguese and *paulista* communities in the region.[4] The new settlers weakened alliances between the indigenous nations. But, Guaná subgroups gradually established different kinds of cooperative relations with the Portuguese (Ladeira & Azanha, 2021).

The Paraguayan War (1864–1870) boosted the systematic occupation of indigenous territories in mid-West Brazil.[5] After the conflict, many combatants of demobilized Brazilian and Paraguayan troops found favorable conditions to stay in the region and establish the ranches that came to characterize it. As a result of that movement, the territory was further Westernized. For the Guaná groups, especially the Terena, this meant coming into added contact with a slave economy and paying a high price (Cardoso de Oliveira, 1976).

The ambitious and adventurous spirit of the war veterans made them an ideal instrument for the State to occupy and explore the lands that today are Mato Grosso do Sul. However, these settlers knew nothing about the importance of the Guaná for the expansion and maintenance of that territory as part of Brazil and had come from other regions where attitudes toward Amerindian peoples – the *bugres* – were disdainful and hostile.[6] The Amerindians on their part were surprised by the predatory character of the settlers, the *purutuyé*, and reached out for the support of the authorities of

58 *Perspectives on consumption (fieldwork experiences)*

Cuiabá, which up to that point had always treated them with the courtesy and respect that allies deserve.[7] Despite complaints, the living conditions of indigenous groups deteriorated (Ladeira & Azanha, 2021).

According to the Terena, the postwar period is the time of servitude. Settlers intensified the establishment of cattle ranches in lands made "available" by the imperial government of Brazil. The dispersed Guaná subgroups sought to reunite and reestablish their villages after the conflict, but now had to ask the new "landowners" for permission to stay in the region. Ultimately, they were cornered into working for the farm owners (Ladeira & Azanha, 2021).

In the early twentieth century, the Terena's situation worsened with the arrival of the Northwest railroad of Brazil (NOB). It took almost ten years of construction work until both ends of the railroad, one coming from Baurú and the other from Porto Esperança, were joined in 1914. From demographic and economic points of view, the NOB brought "progress" to the region. Like the already existing farms, new immigrant settlements became production hubs that attracted the Terena and Guaná peoples in general as workhands. If considering the size and diversity of populations in the territories it crossed, NOB is one of the railroads that most drastically affected indigenous peoples' lives in the world. Non-indigenous population in the region of Mato Grosso do Sul multiplied by five in just two decades (Ladeira & Azanha, 2021).

The Terena found a lifeline in the expeditions of the Rondon Commission, the military operation headed by Marshal Cândido Rondon to expand the telegraph system into the Amazonian region.[8] The visit of the Rondon Commission, which happened before the completion of the railroad, was crucial for guaranteeing the bits of land that the government would turn into Terena reservations. However, the same did not happen for other indigenous peoples that ended up taking refuge in Terena villages, like the Kinikináu. At the turn of the century, ethnocide was a well-oiled destruction machine set in motion against the Guaná groups. The pieces of land the Terena reclaimed through the support of the Telegraph Commission were all they had to start building some form of resistance. The villages of Brejão and Buriti were founded in 1904 and 1922 and confirmed as indigenous reservations in 1922 and 1928, respectively (Cardoso de Oliveira, 1976, p. 60).

Marshal Rondon was the first director of the Indian Protection Service (SPI), the government agency he helped create in 1910. Former members of the Rondon Commission joined the SPI, acting as supervisors of the Terena reservations. In the 1920s, the SPI placed agents in stations in indigenous territories with the purpose of offering "fraternal protection" to the Amerindian peoples, as defended by Marshal Rondon. However, the work of SPI supervisors soon shifted from the protection of indigenous rights to an ideological imposition that deprived the Terena of their autonomy. Station chiefs began interfering in every aspect of Terena life,

Against capital 59

mediating their relations with neighbor farm owners, controlling the uses of their land, and ultimately shaping the conditions for their future in the region. In other words, local government agents who were supposed to be "protectors" of indigenous peoples exerted coercive power over them (Ladeira & Azanha, 2021).

To a large extent, SPI agents played a central role in turning the Terena into workforce supply for agribusiness in Mato Grosso do Sul. As legitimate representatives of the Brazilian State, they used their authority to recruit Terena men and women for work outside the indigenous reservations. By the 1950s, only 19 of 127 domestic groups in the Cachoeirinha village lived exclusively of agriculture and handicrafts done inside Terena land. Almost 60 of them depended on external employments. The rest combined work on their crops with occasional gigs outside (Cardoso de Oliveira, 1968).

When I visited the Terena, 80 years had passed since the founding of the village of Brejão. Near it, there was a second village called Água Branca. From inside the reservation, one could reach Nioaque through smaller back lanes without needing to use the main road. In fact, the reservation's pathways and the city's limits were almost indistinguishable. Borders were unclear, and the change from Terena to Nioaque homes and streets was subtle. Hence, the sign on the main road that marked the "entrance" of the reservation and forbade access to "strangers" had little operational value. Nioaque periphery and indigenous territory were almost the same thing. By the standards of classic interethnic contact theories, the Terena were integrated. They had dissolved as completely into national society as did their reservation in the city's edge.

My argument here, however, is that the Terena cultural identity exists and resists. The Terena's resistance manifests itself precisely through denying the criteria that sustain classic notions of contact and integration. From the standpoint of national society, to which "the economy" is a dominant sphere presiding over every aspect of life, "contact" is foremost about economic measures and relationships. The Terena people seem integrated according to the national society's economic criteria. Darcy Ribeiro (1979) explains that perspective as follows:

> Indigenous populations of modern Brazil can be classified in four categories related to the degree of contact with national society, namely: isolated, intermittent contact, permanent contact, and integrated. These categories represent successive and necessary stages of the integration of indigenous populations to the national society. Some groups, however, disappear before going through all of them, and each group stays for more or less time in a stage according to the vicissitudes of its relations with the civilized [people], certain cultural characteristics of their own and economic variants of the national society they face.
>
> (p. 432)

60   Perspectives on consumption (fieldwork experiences)

Thus, Amerindians are classified based on their degree of contact, moving from one stage in the scale to the next depending on "vicissitudes," "cultural characteristics," or "economic variants." Vicissitudes here means chance or fortune. Cultural characteristic is a too broad and imprecise category. What seems to have real weight in the classification are the economic variants. In that regard, the Terena have gone through all the stages in the contact scale. They are in the fourth stage, cast as integrated. Ribeiro's description of integrated populations clearly refers to economic variants. Integration does not mean the total assimilation of Amerindians nor their blending into the national society. It means the "other" keeps its ethnic identity but behaves according to institutionalized parameters of the dominant society and has an increasing presence in its economic life. In Ribeiro's words, "integrated" indigenous people survived all sorts of compulsions and lived insulated amidst the national population, incorporated in the economy as workforce reserve or as specialized producers of certain types of goods:

> (...) they live enclosed in portions of their ancient territories, or if stripped of their lands, wander from one place to another. Some of these groups lost their original languages, and, apparently, nothing distinguishes them from the rural population with which they live. Equally mixed-race, wearing the same clothes, eating the same food, they could be mistaken for their neo-Brazilian neighbors if they were not sure that they constitute a people apart, did not maintain a kind of loyalty to that ethnic identity, and were not defined, seen, and discriminated against as "Indians" by the surrounding population.
>
> (Ribeiro, 1979, p. 432)

At first glance, the Terena people seem to fit that description. They dress like Brazilians, eat like Brazilians, work in the region's ranches, are mixed-race, speak Portuguese, wander from one place to another. Nothing distinguishes them if looking at these aspects. But, they also see themselves and are seen as "Indians." They are loyal to their ethnic identity and are sure they make up a "people apart." The point that inspires reflection is precisely that strange alchemy of being and not being. What is the logic of that paradox? How can one look like a Brazilian and be a Terena? Was that just stereotyping or stigmatization? On what grounds do they hold on to their ethnic identity?

My purpose, therefore, is to go beyond that definition of "integration," which comes from the national society's point of view. I aim to understand the perspective of the Terena by dodging the economic variants. They have a strategy, a discipline, a knowledge that mitigates their asymmetrical relationship with hegemonic culture. They found leeway to negotiate some of the fundamental pillars for belonging to the national society. In fact, their denial of a fundamental pillar is what constitutes alterity. They want to set themselves apart. Their strategy for establishing the positivity of Terena identity is not introjecting the same rules and central values that define existence in national society, which is a capitalist society.

Against capital 61

In order to examine the Terena's case, I will first discuss central ideological axes of modern Western society. These axes are like cultural markers from which the Terena try to distance themselves to preserve their own identity. Then, I will move on to the analysis of two fieldwork experiences that offer clues for understanding how the Terena people resist ethnocide.

3 The resistance

The Terena reaffirm themselves as an ethnic group by rejecting important features of the dominant culture. It is important to discuss these features to understand how they mark their difference. To be a "people apart" means to experience the opposition between "us" and "them," "our" society and "theirs." It means holding on to that which reveals the difference. By maintaining the contrast, they eschew the ethnocidal process that threatens them systematically and relentlessly. That seems to be the point of view of the Terena, the logical core of their experience of being and wanting to be a people other than just Brazilians.

We will reflect on that logic, seeking clues that indicate what can be most fundamentally rejected from modern capitalist societies (Velho, 1981, p. 16). Resistance against ethnocide requires the refusal to assume what is essential in the "other," betting against points that if removed can dismantle the meaning of the social system conducting the destructive machine. A resistance strategy is knowing what would be unnegotiable as a counterpoint to the "other's" society. Clothing, habitation, everyday practices, and even the foreign language can be elements for negotiation. The point is knowing how much to compromise without disappearing in the other. What is and is not negotiable in resisting ethnocide? Where could the Terena draw a line?

To uncover the terms of that negotiation, I will discuss now four necessary axes of Western modernity: individualism, historicism, the State, and capitalism. Evidently, a thorough examination of these concepts would exceed the limits of this chapter. I wish, however, to stress that these axes define Western society as we know it. Hence, I will discuss these concepts, speculating about possibilities for resistance to Westernization and exploring their meanings against the backdrop of events and discourses I was able to follow during fieldwork. This way, I aim to show how resistance to cultural characteristics derived from these axes can be a way to differentiate, preserve, or construct an ethnic identity.

The notion of "State society" is a standard that separates opposite types of social organization. In the text "Freedom, misfortune, the unnamable," Pierre Clastres examines the issue of voluntary servitude in La Boétie's thought and clearly emphasizes that opposition:

All social machines that function without power relations will be considered primitive societies. Consequently, all societies whose functioning

62   *Perspectives on consumption (fieldwork experiences)*

implies, however minimally it may seem to us, the exercise of power will be considered a so-called State society. In Boétian terms, societies before or after the misfortune. It goes without saying that the universal essence of the State is not realized in a uniform manner in all State formations, the variety of which history shows us. Only in contrast to primitive societies – societies without a State – are all others revealed to be equivalent.

(Clastres, 1980/2010, p. 176)

A State society created roots in Brazil since the Portuguese Crown took over the territory. Its dominance over other societies living in Brazilian land was intensified in the nineteenth century with the transfer of the Royal Family to Rio de Janeiro in 1808 and the subsequent events of the Declaration of Independence in 1822 and the Proclamation of the Republic in 1889. Societies based on the State, a specific conception of power and politics, have trouble dealing with differences. They refuse multiplicity and have a vocation for producing the identical. When a State society articulates itself with capitalism – a specific regime of economic production – differences and alterity become almost unbearable.

For Pierre Clastres, a society that combines the State and capitalism is fatal for others. That combination promotes the absolute intolerance that is behind ethnocide, the destructive machine against difference. A path for resisting the ethnocidal process is to set up defenses that mitigate its effects. The Terena's case illustrates that defensive mechanism, as we will analyze ahead. But first, I want to expand on the other meanings and possible outcomes of a State society.

In Clastres's words, State societies tend to produce the identical, the One. They tend to construct themselves at the center of the social body, equally distant to a group of equals. Hence, the idea of the individual – the equal, by definition – is constitutive to the State society model. Comparing Indian society, founded on the principle of hierarchy, to the West, Dumont (1972, p. 38) says:

> Our two cardinal ideals are called equality and liberty. They assume as their common principle, and as a valorized representation, the idea of the human *individual*: humanity is made up of men, and each man is conceived as presenting, in spite of and over and above his particularity, the essence of humanity.

Therefore, a State society produces equals, and builds and underlines the identical. It is a society where the individual as a principal articulates ideas of liberty and equality. State and individual are interrelated, juxtaposed elements that arrange a particular way of being in society. Modern Western society carries both these axes coupled with other two: historicism and the capitalist model of economic production.

Against capital 63

Historical perspective provides the basis for weaving the becoming of events. The axis of historicism interlaces episodes in a permanent forward-moving impulse. Like the State, historicism is a frontier between societies, an all-embracing theory in the West not espoused by indigenous thought. Reflecting on that frontier aspect, Lévi-Strauss (1976) argues the following:

> The question is not knowing whether the societies called "primitive" have or do not have a history in the sense we give this term. These societies exist in time like all the others, and with the same title to it, but unlike us, they refuse to belong to history and they try very hard to inhibit, within themselves, whatever would constitute the faint promise of a historical development. (...) Our Western societies are made for change; it is the principle of their structure and of their organization. The societies called "primitive" appear to us to be such mostly because they have been conceived by their members to endure. (...) Nothing is left to chance in them, and the double principle that there is a place for everything, that everything must be in its place, permeates moral and social life. It also explains how societies with a very low techno-economic level can experience a feeling of well-being and plenitude, and how each of them believes it offers its members the only life worth living.
>
> (pp. 321–322)

The refusal of history and the State distinguish indigenous groups in a double opposition to the modern West, characterized by the acceptance of these ideas. Both Pierre Clastres and Lévi-Strauss emphasize – one through the State, the other through historicism – a clear-cut difference between indigenous and Western societies. The question of the individual as a core value is another possible differentiation. Establishing dichotomies that seem to permeate an indefinite set of situations is always a delicate approach, and we should see them only as a heuristic possibility for interpreting concrete experiences of the relationship between different societies.

In this framework of axes that characterize Western society and may be thought of as markers of differentiation, we can add the regime of economic production. Here, the differences between worlds are exacerbated and the evidence of tension is even clearer. The point is that societies that refuse historicism and the State also refuse the economy. In Brazil, indigenous societies that refuse or, to the limit, are against the economy are compelled to live in contact with the Westernized world, which bases its existence on the economic perspective, on the notions of "production" and "productivity" that occupy a central place in its imagination and in the organization of its experiences and social practices. Clastres's also refers to Sahlin's seminal work to discuss the meaning of economy for indigenous societies:

> The ethnographically founded claim that on the one hand, primitive economies are underproductive (only a segment of society works for

64 Perspectives on consumption (fieldwork experiences)

short periods of time at low intensity), that on the other, they always satisfy the needs of society (needs defined by the society itself and not by an exterior example), such a claim then imposes, in its paradoxical truth, the idea that primitive society is, indeed, a society of abundance (certainly the first, perhaps also the last), since all needs are satisfied. But it also summons the logic at the heart of this social system: *structurally*, writes Sahlins, *"economy" does not exist*. That is to say that the economic, as a sector unfolding autonomously in the social arena, is absent from the DMP; the latter functions as consumer production (to assure the satisfaction of needs) and not as production of exchange (to acquire profit by commercializing surplus goods). What is clear, finally (what Sahlins' great work asserts), is the discovery that primitive societies are societies that refuse economy.

(Clastres, 1980/2010, pp. 197–198)

Marshall Sahlins' (1972/2017) work interprets indigenous societies as societies that refuse economic thought. This refusal becomes evident when they come in contact with Western societies that build their realities entirely from the economic perspective, especially capitalism. For the capitalist system, the world is foremost usable and necessarily productive. Nothing in it is impossible in terms of production. Its logic is that of industry. The economy is centered on utilitarian thought. Resource exploitation is its rule. Everything should be useful and active; inactivity, unproductivity, and unusefulness are unbearable in capitalist societies. The inevitable consequence is the devastation of other societies it encounters in its path of expansion by genocide, ethnocide, or both. Ethnocide, therefore, is a matter of the State, which does not tolerate difference, and the economy, to which existence only finds meaning in production:

What differentiates the West is capitalism, as the impossibility of remaining within a frontier, as the passing beyond of all frontiers; it is capitalism as a system of production for which nothing is impossible, unless it is not being an end in itself: whether liberal, private, as in Western Europe, or planned of the State, as in Eastern Europe. Industrial society, the most formidable machine of production, is for that very reason the most terrifying machine of destruction. Races, societies, individuals; space, nature, seas, forests, subsoils: everything is useful, everything must be used, everything must be productive, with productivity pushed to its maximum rate of intensity.

(Clastres, 1980/2010, p. 112)

This is the irreversible point. Integration into Brazilian society is the terminal phase of the abovementioned four grades of contact. Beyond integration would be, like Darcy Ribeiro said, to become an indistinguishable

Against capital 65

part, a fusion, total group assimilation. It would be the completion of the destructive enterprise of ethnocide. In the Terena's case, there is resistance. They are still Terena despite their degree of "integration." The question is: why should we understand the contact between societies that have such radically opposite conceptions of the economy precisely from the economic perspective of one of them? Or, better yet, how can the Terena or any other indigenous society have its degree of contact measured in terms of an economic variable? How does the economy of Western society measures others' integration? Possibly, the strategy to be Terena is preserving the radically different notion of economy. The Terena continue to see themselves as indigenous people because they do not share the same ideas of economy, work, utilitarianism, and productivity as the Brazilians, who regard them as "outdated" or "primitives." Therefore, understanding the existing problems of contact through the experiences, categories, and concepts of Brazilian national society is questionable.

That was the aspect that caught my attention in the interactions I had with the Terenas and the farm owners while staying in Mato Grosso do Sul back in 1985. Specifically, two experiences – one with members of the indigenous community and another with the farm owners – showed me how the difference in economic notions separates the Terena from national society. Coexistence with the difference is difficult for modern Western societies, where the forces of the State, historicism, individualism, and capitalism come into play. There is no room in them for alternatives. Their characteristic is to exclude. Peoples that diverge from them do so with the intent, implicit or explicit, of postponing their exclusion. By silently refusing core Western values and bearing with the resulting contradictions in their daily lives, indigenous societies make their way to survival. The Terena's existence today, despite 300 years of contact, suggests that they have a well-woven, ingenious, and successful strategy.

In the remainder of this chapter, I will discuss the two situations that, in my interpretation, reveal the Terena have a specific way of dealing with the "regional economy" that helps them strengthen their cultural identity. I do not attempt to make a comprehensive study of the Terena's strategy and how they cope with the forces of the State, individualism, and historicism. My focus is on the different relationship the indigenous people have with the practices and principles that define modern capitalism.

4 Two experiences in Nioaque

The two episodes I chose to discuss in this chapter are exemplary of the opposite attitudes and thoughts the Terena and the ranch owners have on the "regional economy." These were not extraordinary events in any way. There was no explicit conflict, tension, or argument between both groups. There was no dispute over a specific object and no one, except me, gave them much thought. These were ordinary situations that likely happen on a

66 Perspectives on consumption (fieldwork experiences)

frequent basis. Through careful consideration, however, I realized that the agents involved had different understandings of the economic world.

I take these episodes as representatives of the contrast between the "indigenous" and the "national" perspectives on the local economy precisely because of their unexceptional, everyday character. My argument is that the Terena's divergence from the dominant national logic is an important factor in their resistance against ethnocide. This is my interpretation of the specific experience of the Terena in Mato Grosso do Sul based on my fieldwork in 1985. The analysis of their case is relevant today at least for three different reasons. First and foremost, the Terena population continues to exist and has grown in the past three decades, despite the persistent hostility of parcels of national society against indigenous peoples. Second, the dominance of the Western capitalist perspective still perpetuates mistaken beliefs in everyday about the so-called integration of indigenous peoples based on economic criteria, particularly consumption signifiers, such as clothes, cars, cell phones, electronic gadgets, and so on. Third, these misconceptions continue to be weaponized in political discourse to justify measures against indigenous rights and interests.

The strength of both episodes as objects of analysis lies in their simplicity and ordinariness. They are illustrative because they are so common in that social universe. Everyone said and did things they knew and were used to saying and doing. No one was revealing any secrets. The emphasis was on naturalness. In these situations, I could clearly identify the existence of two separate logics, opposing desires, and very different ways of seeing what was at stake.

The first episode was a long, after-dinner conversation among friends, in-between cigarettes and coffee. The owner of a ranch next to the Terena reservation had invited me over to his house. The conversation touched on business, jobs, salaries, income, investments in lands, ranching, cattle. These were predictable conversation topics in that place and for those participants.

The other episode was also a long conversation, but at the house of a Terena family, between the hosts and a group of Brazilian tourists from Rio de Janeiro. It was not unusual for the Terena to have "white" guests in the reservation coming from Nioaque and the neighboring farms. Normally, they would offer visitors a glass of water or a cup of coffee. It was common to see indigenous and "white" individuals sitting together and talking at *bolichos*, at the doorsteps of their houses, below the cool shade of a tree. These encounters were predominantly slow, unrushed, according to the local atmosphere. Tourists in the region would often want to buy bows, arrows, and necklaces as souvenirs.

The situations reveal a stark contrast between the non-indigenous' and the Terena's view of the economy. The Terena were classified as "integrated" according to the capitalist perspective on the "regional economy" and judged by their neighbor farm owners according to capitalist standards.

Against capital 67

It is also the Terena's (mostly discreet) attitude against capitalism – their refusal to participate in the economy as non-indigenous agents would expect them to – that defines them as a people apart.

***

The meals at the ranch happened in three well-defined spaces. Overseers, ranch hands (many of them Terena), and house employees ate in scheduled hours, at the sound of the bell, on a large table placed away from the main house. The table was set in a kind of porch that surrounded the dwelling of the principal employees. The ranch's owners, their relatives, and guests had meals in two spaces in the main house. Breakfast was on the balcony, lunch and dinner were in the dining room. There were 11 people present at the dinner in question: the ranch's owner and his wife, their engineer son, a young male farmer, a female business manager, a female school teacher, two teenagers, two small kids, and myself.

After dinner, the conversation topic emerges naturally because the hosts had invited the young farmer – let's call him Carlos – over for business. Carlos was staying overnight to see lands and cattle the next morning and close a deal with José, the host. The young man was born in a nearby region. In his mid to late 20s, he was experiencing an ascending economic trajectory. Specifically, he had grown rich over the past four or five years when, according to him, he stopped being a "boy." The host defined him as "go-getter," "hardworking," and "a young man of worth" on several opportunities.

When Carlos was about 20 years old, he sold his car, motorcycle, and some stocks. With the money, he bought cattle, around 30 steers to be fattened for slaughter, but had no land. So, he leased a piece of idle farmland and arranged with the owner that he would develop the area within two years. Developing land is laborious and costly work. It means to fence the entire perimeter, prune shrubs, prepare water fountains for the livestock, divide pastures, build cowsheds, corrals, warehouses, houses, and a series of other support structures. Plus, there are all the tasks of vaccinating, feeding, breeding, and selling the livestock. In his words, he worked from sunrise to sunrise, with his own hands, immersed up to the neck in all the mess.

Carlos was very proud of his beginnings, which almost cost him his marriage. His wife did not adapt to life in the country and decided to go back to her parents' house in Campo Grande. As a result of his initial efforts, he made a lot of money, leased other lands, bought more cattle. When we met at the dinner, his wife was expecting their first child and still lived in the city. He wanted a boy, a male heir that would become a farm owner like himself.

It was Carlos who started the conversation with compliments to the hosts' lands and cattle. He talked about the wealth generated by all the farms. The food we ate at dinner, noted José, had been produced at the ranch.

68   *Perspectives on consumption (fieldwork experiences)*

The engineer son, however, said that it was possible to live better, make more money, acquire more property, and get opportunities in the big cities. Both farmers vehemently disagreed, raising the temperature of the conversation. The three women made few interventions commenting on the relationship between "money" and "sacrifice." They saw country life as demanding many "sacrifices" and giving back little possibilities to "enjoy the money." While the engineer son agreed with them, Carlos and José had a hard time assimilating that different point of view. The friendly but heated debate revolved around a central question – "where are the best chances for getting rich?" – and an understanding – the certainty that the right way to live is the one that leads to making more money. This tacit agreement came up constantly during the evening, because the interlocutors discussed the country/city opposition in terms of opportunities for working hard, earning wealth, and "making it."

I was just quietly listening to them when they started to tease me with the old story that teachers are always on "vacation." In response, the school teacher gave a long and enthusiastic speech about the huge responsibilities of education professionals, who receive meager financial compensations for their job. Everyone agreed to that, so I took advantage of the pause to ask what they thought about the reservation and the life of their neighbor Terenas. The farmers' view was so in sync that my impression was that I had given José and Carlos the cue for saying their rehearsed lines. Their tone of indignation was such that it seemed like someone had robbed them. The words they most used were "waste," *"politicagem"* ("political favor"), and "madness." Overall, their opinion was that to preserve the Terena's territory was like to "throw away" good lands that could be "better used" for the benefit of Brazil. It was "idleness in a country that is so poor and destitute." The "Indians" were "laidback" and "wanted nothing to do with work": they were "vagrants," "lazy," and *"malandros."*[9] The engineer, coherent with his detached image of the indigenous peoples (Cardoso de Oliveira, 1972), tried to relativize the matter a bit.

I asked about the performance of the Terena I had met and seen working at the ranch. José acknowledged they were good on some tasks, but usually worked on contract and not as regular hands. They worked for a fixed period, got paid, and left. That was their preferred way of doing things. They wanted to receive payment and be on their way as quickly as possible. When the money was over, they came back for another contract. As steady employees, José said, they were unreliable and did not last long in the job. To give an example of the Terenas' "indifference," the host recalled that one them had made a big mess earlier that day mixing some marked head of cattle in a herd of unmarked cattle, costing everyone a lot of time to sort them out. The Terena "wanted nothing," did not think about "moving up in life" because they had "no ambition."

Carlos was in favor of the end of the indigenous reservation so the lands could become economically productive, generating wealth and jobs.

Against capital 69

The Terena's "indolence" and the "non-use" of so many acres were unacceptable to him. His opinion set the tone of the rest of the debate on that topic. At a certain point, Carlos talked about postponing his desire to buy a new pickup truck because of the expenses he and his wife were having to remodel their house for the baby's arrival. His remark shifted the conversation theme to consumption, inspiring the hosts and other guests to give him all sorts of shopping advice on cars, furniture, and baby-related products. We finished drinking our coffees on the balcony and said goodnight.

***

The second episode had different characters and setting. The theme – money and business – was, to some extent, similar, but because of the nature of the interaction itself, not the flow of the conversation. It was a pretty common situation for the Terena. A group of tourists, two white couples and their respective kids, who were guests at one of the region's ranches, visited the reservation. Antonio, an employee at the ranch who knew the Terena well, drove them there. The specific purpose of their visit was to find a Terena who was an expert in making bows, arrows, necklaces, and wooden artifacts (bowls, mortars, pestles, etc.) and was willing to sell them. Luís Terena was their guide in the reservation, and I tagged along.

Following Luís's advice, we knocked on the door of specific houses to try and do business with the craftsmen who lived in them. There were very few Terena that Luís judged to be up to the task of making – and selling – those "typical" artifacts. The quality of the handcrafts had to be worthy of the Terena. In his words, "very few still know how to do these things well."

The first two attempts were unsuccessful. The female residents greeted us with kindness, but the conversations were brief because their husbands were unavailable. The husband from the first home was "out," the second was in Nioaque. In both cases, the wives were sorry for their husbands' absence and remarked that "nowadays, it is very hard to find someone who makes these objects."

At last, the third attempt felt promising. By a muddy track was a construction made of wood that, according to the sign on the door and the cross, was a small church. Next to it was the narrow shortcut we took to Cisto Terena's house. Inside, his wife was expecting us. The children ran excited toward Luís. Like in the other two homes, there were dogs, lots of bugs, and scorching sun. But this one had a small unpaved front yard with no trees. The house's floor was also unpaved. There was no front wall. So, only the shadow of the roof broke the continuity between inside and outside. Luckily, Cisto was in the crops just out the back of the house. While one of his small children went to "fetch" him, all of us visitors and the wife sat down on the wood benches to wait.

Luís explained the tourists were looking to buy necklaces, bracelets, bow and arrow, and so on as souvenirs from the Terena village. Cisto's wife said

70 Perspectives on consumption (fieldwork experiences)

he was very skillful at making those things but had nothing ready at that moment. The last time he sold a bow and arrow had been a long time ago and to a friend who was leaving the region. Very carefully and slowly, she stretched her arms and pulled two half-done bows from a board propped between two beams in the ceiling. Her husband, she explained, crafted the artifacts unhurriedly. He had started work on the one that was closest to completion six months ago. One of the tourists' kids asked if Cisto could speed up and finish those bows on that same day so they could buy them. The wife smiled, and Luís stood up to talk to Cisto, who was walking inside right at that instant.

I was impressed by the rhythm of words being exchanged, the restraint and stiffness of dialogues, the formality of introductions, the arrangement of people in their seats, the calmness of gestures. The interaction seemed to be in "slow-motion." My subjective feeling found some objectivity and external expression in the signs of impatience the kid tourists – and, less explicitly, their parents – were giving out. The pace of that meeting was nothing like the shopping scenes of major urban centers. There were no products with price tags on shelves or in display windows. Nothing recalled the experience of shopping malls, supermarkets, or even the small Guaikurú handcrafts shop at the airport of Campo Grande. In fact, there were no eager salespeople. Though we were there to buy, Cisto and his wife did not seem at all concerned with selling. Their apparent lack of effort to make the sale was also not a strategy to up the price. Neither it was rudeness nor contempt. The conversation was cheerful, and everyone involved was pleasant and polite.

The conversation drifted to various topics unrelated to the purpose of the visit. Suddenly, one of the tourists decided to ask if it would be possible to buy some Terena souvenirs. They were from Rio de Janeiro and were heading back to their city in a few days. Cisto looked at the tourist, the wife, the other couple, and their kids. After a long silence, he said that yes, it was possible. He did not, however, ask the tourists what they wished to buy. Neither did he comment on price or delivery.

So, the tourists explained they wanted a bow and arrow, three bracelets, and two necklaces. Was it possible to do all that within just a few days? "Yes," Cisto replied. Was it a lot of work? Yes, it was. Could he make necklaces and bracelets? Yes, if the wife helped him. Would the wife help? Smiles, hesitations, pauses. Would she? Yes, she would! And, how much would they charge? Would it be expensive? "I don't know... I don't know the price," Cisto said. Neither did the tourists. A long silence followed. Would you like bracelets made of beads or *Angola*, Cisco asked. What is the difference? The craftsman pointed with his chin toward the hens out in the front yard to explain the meaning of *Angola*.[10] Then, he went behind a curtain into another room and came back with a plastic bag filled with beads. He spilled the beads over the table and played with them. The tourists loved the beautiful beads. They wanted necklaces made of beads

Against capital 71

and bracelets made of feathers or whatever other combination Cisto liked best. But then the craftsman would "need more time to decide." Since the tourists did not have much time, they made up their minds and sorted out the items made of beads and feathers. How much would the adornments cost? How much were the bow and arrow? Once again, the memory of the last friend to buy the items popped up in the conversation. Silence. Cisto was absorbed in his thoughts while staring at the half-done bow. He came to no conclusion about the price. How much had the friend paid? He did not know. "Do you remember, woman?" She thought it was 20 something. Finally, after some more discussion, the tourists and Cisto reached an understanding. They were paying 70 for the entire order. Everyone seemed pleased. One of the tourists asked if Cisto wanted the money upfront. Cisto calmly replied that payment in advance was not necessary and then distracted himself looking at something outside.

Two of the tourists looked at their watches simultaneously, while Cisto and Luís looked at the field. Everyone stood up and started saying their goodbyes. The arrangement was that Cisto would deliver the objects through Luís the day before the tourists' departure. Luís would take the objects to the ranch and deliver the payment to Cisto the next day. It was all settled. The tourists were grateful. The meeting was over. The kids expressed a bit of frustration with going back to the ranch empty-handed. One of the mothers reiterated they would have their souvenirs in a couple of days. Still, the visit to the Terena was not the shopping experience the kids had expected.

Outside, the sun was brutal. As we took the shortcut back to the church, Antonio asked if the tourists had not noticed his signs suggesting them to pay only 50 for everything. They had not. But they did not mind paying a little bit more. "It really makes no difference," Antonio said, changing his mind. "Cisto won't make the objects, Luís won't show up, and you won't pay a thing." According to Antonio, the one-hour meeting had been a waste of time. "They," the Terena, "don't care about earning some money." They "don't care about anything."

Antonio was right about the outcome of that business deal. Luís did not show on the day set for the delivery. A few days later, I learned that Cisto had not even begun making the objects.

***

These two experiences do not authorize any kind of generalization about the opposite relationships of indigenous and Western cultures with the economic world. They provide initial evidence about the different perspectives of the Terena on one side and capitalist society, embodied by the ranch owners, on the other, and the former's refusal to fully submit to the values and practices of the latter. The questions of cultural difference, interethnic contact, ethnocide, and resistance involve many complex elements.

72 *Perspectives on consumption (fieldwork experiences)*

These episodes suggest that resisting capitalism is one of the crucial elements preserving the Terena as a people apart. Being Terena and persisting as such involves many dimensions, including, as the situations described above show, an attitude against patterns that are fundamental to capitalist society.

Effective resistance to ethnocide is related to the effectiveness in affirming alterity and denying belonging. In his fieldwork, Cardoso de Oliveira (1976) recorded the case of a Terena man who got rich and incited the hostility of his group. The direct relationship between the group's hostility and the man's financial gains indicates the Terena rejected more individualist – and capitalist – projects. Similarly, the point of the situations I examined in this chapter is also that the Terena do not meet capitalist expectations. Their seeming "unfitness" for work and business suggests they have a different understanding of their so-called integration in the regional economy.

There are many elements to consider in the ongoing contact between indigenous and non-indigenous cultures in Brazil. For instance, there is the issue of the penetration of Christian religions in indigenous territories, especially with the growing presence of evangelical organizations (Vilaça, 2014, 2015; Acçolini, 2015; Leite, 2018). Religious affiliations among the Terena was a delicate topic, possibly because of stereotypes external to the reservation. The evangelicals, known as *crentes*, were associated to the images of "workers" and "honest people" as opposed to the images of *cachaceiros* or "drunkards" and "vagabonds" of non-evangelicals.[11] On multiple occasions, I heard that only Protestant Terenas were "good on the job" because the others wanted nothing to do with "work" or even "making and saving money." Cardoso de Oliveira (1976, p. 101) had already observed that way of classifying and stereotyping the Terena based on religious affiliations in the 1950s.

Since the "protestant ethic" stresses the values of work, entrepreneurship, and production (Weber, 1904/2001), one could assume that the refusal of capitalism as a strategy of resistance is more characteristic of predominantly non-evangelical villages or groups. However, Acçolini's (2015) work shows the conversion to Protestantism among the Terena is not a straight-forward, uncomplicated process. The Terena do not simply accept the Christian faith but adapt and transform some of its elements according to their own culture. Acçolini (2015) calls this translation process the "*terenization* of Protestantism." Tracing the history of evangelicals among the Terena, the author discusses how they took over a branch of a protestant organization called the Union of the Evangelical Churches of South America after ending their relationship with north-American missionaries of the South American Indian Mission (SAIM) in the early 1990s. Among the many problems that led to that break up were disagreements regarding money and accounting. The north-Americans wanted receipts and the bookkeeping of payments and proceeds. The Terena were not used to dealing with money in that way and did not comply with the rigorous accounting demands of SAIM.

Against capital 73

This chapter reflected on the survival of the Terena amidst Brazilian national society. The Terena's assimilation into the dominant culture and their extinction as a people did not happen. They continue to be "a people apart," they have not succumbed to the ethnocidal process even if the odds were against them. Their endurance results from many factors and internal strategies. My argument here is that one of these strategies involves the refusal of core values and patterns of the national society's way of life, the denial of a productivist, moneymaking view of the world. The Terena's reluctance against the productivity standards of capitalism marks their difference. In this sense, there is a third way for indigenous populations to deal with national society other than the "combative" and "docile" attitudes that Darcy Ribeiro (1979, p. 438) mentions. These two attitudes point to the same destiny: the dissolution of cultural identity. The combative alternative often leads to genocide; the docile enables ethnocide. The Terena's case suggests there is another way of facing national society – a wise and patient way – that allows them to escape destruction, even if barely. They negotiate contact to the degree that does not mean their disappearance into the "other." The three centuries of resistance against ethnocide taught Terena society that the refusal of economic thought is not just a way of being but of preventing the annulment of their identity.

Notes

1 I changed all names to pseudonyms to protect my interlocutors' privacy. Indigenous people have for long used the names of their ethnic groups as their last name. However, it was only in 2012 that a resolution guaranteed their right to register their ethnic name in birth certificates and official ID documents. See http://www.funai.gov.br/index.php/docb/registro-civil-de-nacimento-rcn.
2 For most of the twentieth century, official Brazilian policies and legislation regarding indigenous peoples had as an underlying premise the idea of assimilation. Indigenous peoples were under State tutelage until their full integration into national society. This situation began to change in a positive direction only with the 1988 Federal Constitution, which acknowledges and determines indigenous rights, including their right to land.
3 *Bolichos* are small bars or markets located in busy spots, near the main roads, or in streets inside the farms where local workers regularly meet and have endless conversations.
4 *Paulista* as in from São Paulo.
5 During my time in Nioaque, I saw a sign honoring the efforts of soldiers in the episode known as the Laguna retreat. This episode was also memorialized by the Viscount of Taunay's (1874) work.
6 *Bugre* is how European colonizers called the "heretic" indigenous men and women in Brazil.
7 *Purutuyé* means the Portuguese or white non-indigenous peoples in general.
8 In Brazil, Marshal is a five-star army rank. Currently, the Brazilian army grants five-star ranks only during wartime.
9 *Malandros* are typical characters in Brazilian imagination. They are creative, bohemian, fun, and idle men who twist rules and laws to their favor. In this case, *malandro* emphasizes idleness and the aversion to productivity.

74   *Perspectives on consumption (fieldwork experiences)*

10 The guinea fowl is called *galinha-d'angola* in Brazil. *Angola* meant hen feathers.
11 In Brazil, members of various protestant denominations are generically called *crentes* or "believers." *Cachaceiro* means a person who drinks a lot of *cachaça* or any kind of liquor.

References

Acçolini, G. (2015). *Protestantismo à moda* Terena. UFGD.

Cardoso de Oliveira, R. (1968). *Urbanização e tribalismo: A integração dos índios Terena numa sociedade de classes*. Zahar.

Cardoso de Oliveira, R. (Ed.) (1972). *A Sociologia do Brasil Indígena*. Rio de Janeiro: Tempo Brasileiro.

Cardoso de Oliveira, R. (1976). *Do índio ao bugre: O processo de assimilação dos Terena*. Francisco Alves.

Clastres, P. (2010). *Archeology of violence* (J. Herman, Trans.). Semiotext(e). (Original work published 1980).

Dumont, L. (1972). *Homo Hierarchicus: The Caste System and Its Implications* (M. Sainsbury, L. Dumont, & B. Gulati, Trans.). Paladin. (Original work published 1966).

Ladeira, M. E., & Azanha, G. (2021, January 25). Terena, *Povos Indígenas do Brasil*. https://pib.socioambiental.org/pt/Povo:Terena.

Leite, T. (2018). Mudando de ideia: cristianismo evangélico e festas de caxiri entre os Ninam do Alto Mucajaí, *Mana*, 24, 216–246. http://dx.doi.org/10.1590/1678-49442018v24n3p216.

Lévi-Strauss, C. (1952). *Race and History*. UNESCO.

Lévi-Strauss, C. (1976). Cultural discontinuity and economic and social development. In: C. Lévi-Strauss (Ed.), *Structural Anthropology*, volume II (pp. 312–322, M. Layton, Trans.). Basic Books. (Original work published 1973).

Ribeiro, D. (1979). *Os índios e a civilização: A integração das populações indígenas no Brasil moderno*. Vozes.

Rocha, E. (1984). *O que é etnocentrismo*. Brasiliense.

Sahlins, M. (2017). *Stone age economics*. Routledge. (First published 1972).

Taunay, A. d'E. (1874). *A retirada de Laguna*. Typographia Americana.

Velho, G. (1981). *Individualismo e cultura: Notas para uma antropologia da sociedade contemporânea*. Zahar.

Vilaça, A. (2014). Culture and self: The different "gifts" Amerindians receive from Catholics and Evangelicals. *Current Anthropology*, 55(S10), pp. S322–S332. https://doi.org/10.1086/678118.

Vilaça, A. (2015). Do animists become naturalists when converting to Christianity? Discussing an ontological turn. *Cambridge Anthropology*, 33, pp. 3–19. https://doi.org/10.3167/ca.2015.330202.

Weber, M. (2001). *The Protestant Ethic and the Spirit of Capitalism* (T. Parsons, Trans.). Routledge. (Original work published 1904).

Part II
Perspectives on consumption through media images

5 The woman in pieces

Advertising and the construction of feminine identity

1 Communication, advertising, and symbolic systems

This chapter analyzes women's images in Brazilian advertising. Its aim is to understand the logic by which ads elaborate an image of feminine identity, and in that process, transform the woman into a silent and fragmented body. The "woman," like other advertising representations, has by definition the duty to make sales of products and services possible. Every ad needs to maintain a constant and intense dialogue with society, making a very particular cut of the innumerable possibilities opened by the social experiences available. Therefore, I consider the thorough analysis of that material a strategic way of understanding how an ideological pattern of contemporary culture classifies differences between social groups through consumption. In this chapter, I wish to explore the analytical tradition of symbolic anthropology and contribute to the debate concerning social representations in mass communication in general and, particularly, in advertising.

The problem of women's images in the media has been of central concern to researchers of modern Western culture since the twentieth century and up to recent years (McLuhan, 1951; Friedan, 1963/2012; Goffman, 1977; Bordo, 1993; McRobbie, 2009). In the late 2010s, women's fight for equality and against sexual violence gained global momentum under the umbrella of the "Me Too" movement, following Hollywood female actors' accusations against powerful industry leaders for sexual harassment. The movement had repercussions in Brazilian media, recharging the focus on topics concerning women's control over their bodies and the many challenges they face in the job market and social life at large – work-life balance, lack of opportunities for female leadership, unfair earnings, sexual abuse, femicide, and so on. The ads I examine in this chapter were published in Brazilian magazines through the 1980s. That was the decade of the country's re-democratization, a process that began slowly in the late 1970s, leading up to the indirect election in 1985 of the first civilian president after 21 years of military dictatorship. Different movements in favor of labor rights, indigenous peoples' rights, freedom of expression, racial

DOI: 10.4324/9781003176794-7

78 Perspectives on consumption (media images)

justice, and women's liberation, among other causes, participated in the efforts for the return of the democratic regime. Hence, to some extent, the 1980s were an even more effervescent moment in the fight for female empowerment and autonomy in the media, at least on the explicit level of representations.

The themes I approach here – mass communication, social identity, advertising, and culture – are broad and multifaceted. An in-depth discussion of each of them exceeds the limits to this chapter. However, it is important to refer to the issue that relates directly to this chapter which is women's representations in the media and their ideological consequences. Many authors have focused on discussing the feminist perspective, the politics and the power involved in the idealization of women, the uses of female body images for consumption purposes, cultural aspects of gender role portrayals, and the reproduction of patriarchal models in mass communication.[1] Kates and Shaw-Garlock (1999) examine ads in female magazines to analyze ideological representations of women, while Lynn, Hardin, and Walsdorf (2004) investigate photographs of women in sports publications, indicating a sustained support to sexual difference that would serve capitalist hegemony. Also, Kilbourne (2000) studies the impact of ads that target young female consumers, concluding that advertising creates a kind of addictive effect that persuades women to recurrent consumption practices as a path to fulfilling their dreams. In this respect, Banet-Weiser and Portwood-Stacer (2006) point to the construction of a postfeminist consumer that embarks in a project of self-actualization through cosmetic surgeries and diverse beauty treatments, emphasizing ideas of personal choice and individualization instead of original feminist causes of social change and liberation.

Goffman (1977) demonstrates the hyper-ritualization of femininity in advertising by examining hundreds of images of women. His analysis shows ads portray the woman as kind, docile, and playful, constructing her identity with values and labels such as "submissive," "hidden," "distanced," "toy," "childish," "funny," "sweet," and "happy." Moreover, ads attribute fundamental meanings to women through opposition to the world of men, classifying feminine identity in a subordinate hierarchical position. Goffman explains how advertising frequently portrays women in a passive or assistant position, while men often symbolize a superior status and are pictured in a protective attitude, according to the social environment (familial, professional, or affective) where they interact with other participants.

Bearing all of these ideas in mind, this study should be read as part of the tradition of studies on women's images in the media and as an interpretation of a concrete case of advertising construction of feminine identity in Brazil. Its goal is to indicate that anthropology has a distinctive way of analysis that is an important contribution for the dialogue that should characterize research over the immense repertoire of images, identities, representations,

The woman in pieces 79

symbolisms, and classification systems available throughout the so-called culture industry. Generally, people tend to think that everything in the world of media changes rapidly. Advertising always seems so contemporary, modern, new, and bold, or at least in line with the latest cultural trend (whatever that may be). We see advertising as a kind of radar that captures what is up to date, always pretending to indicate social changes. Things, however, are not always what they seem. From a certain perspective, advertising images do identify the change. But from another angle, we see an impressive recurrence in the meanings of such images in various moments. In other words, representations of women – and also of men, children, the family, and so forth – present "novelty without change" (Phillips, 1976). Though ads tend to seem new in form and in style, a careful comparison unveils an amazing similarity between their structural plans. This indicates that they seem to be in what Lévi-Strauss (1962a, 1962b) called totemic temporality – cyclic, nonlinear, a kind of "time" that bets on permanency, and is parted from the historical order. This temporality is an important issue to understand advertising as a speech that classifies objects and people through consumption.

The questions that advertising presents to thought are an interesting challenge for their diversity and complexity. Representations that inhabit collective imagination offer a kind of "script" for us to enact in everyday experiences. In my work, I resort to anthropological theories and tools to interpret the universe of images, ideas, and meanings that pour out of the culture industry (Rocha, 2006, 2010, 2012). I believe there is a lot of potential for intellectual work in following this path of study, especially if we think of the media as one of the most active voices occupying public spaces in contemporary culture. Its messages perform a drama in which meanings are made public, consensus is imposed, and ideologies spread.

The culture industry places society before an extensive repertoire of ideas, emotions, feelings, sensations, choices, and practices. Representations of society form a complex ideological universe which is reflected and transformed by advertisements, newspapers, soap operas, magazines, news broadcasts, films, social media contents, and so on. These representations are like a systematic speech and, from the social actor's point of view, a speech as comfortable as it is inevitable. However, this ideological universe transmitted by mass communication always has consumption as purpose and as a way of self-maintenance. Without consumption, the media system is unfeasible. The commitment to consumption – of products, services, ideas, tastes, and feelings – calls for the use of a common language with the public, because the media only makes sense to the audience. For the media, comprehensibility is a matter of maintenance. Media representations are not unilateral creations, but an exercise over a concrete relationship between performers and audience through a common code. Each product of the media is a bridge that establishes itself with the thoughts and practices of the respective consumer markets.

80 *Perspectives on consumption (media images)*

The relationship between society and the culture industry can be seen as a mirror maze where images duplicate in countless rebounds. The important thing is that whatever the precise form of that relationship, the meanings produced by the media are public, shared, and collective, which makes it hard, for example, for someone not to understand an advertisement, radio news, television program, or newspaper photo. This indicates that the study of meanings propagated through these materials serves as a clue toward the existing models, desires, and dilemmas of a culture. The culture industry raises interest because of the keys it possesses for accessing the imagination of the society that produces it. In this sense, I propose to investigate the most evident traces of what ads show as the feminine identity. More specifically, I examine how women's images in advertising present a fragmented body and a silent being so that products may "speak" for her.

The feelings that are expressed, the privacy that is shown, and the intimacy that is exposed in advertisements are not individual characteristics, but collective representations once publicly exhibited. In Durkheim's (1970) sense, they are social representations: a "thing" that is coercive, extensive, and external to the individual. The identities, both of the "man" and of the "woman," once translated by the media, turn into codes or patterns where society sees ideas, styles, and practices. In this sense, these identities are not a dimension of the individual that hovers beyond the social. When transformed into media images, identities are no longer a "judgment of one's conscience," but a collective classification constituted through likewise social values. The feminine identity constructed in ads does not care for inner selves, subjective characters, or the multiple facets of the psychological universe. Ads do not speak about the difference between individuals or about singularities, because selling is betting on the far-reaching and group discourse, classifying everything that is possible as a consumer public. Advertisements speak of products and services to reach consumers. They are generic to the extent of their markets. The media communicates through what we have in common: collective representations and social classifications.

Thus, I wish to retain two basic points. The first is that this study, paraphrasing Clifford Geertz (1973), is not "about" the culture industry but "in" the culture industry, particularly in advertisements, assuming the symbolic material they propagate necessarily has an intense relationship with society. Ads must exchange with receivers; they cannot be strangers or detached. These materials must fit into the lives of consumers. The second point is that identity is inclusive. It is something that encompasses the individual and annuls its subjective and psychological dimensions. We shall look at identity as a social fact, codified in the media as a behavior model that defines "what is," "what can be," or "what should be" in the feminine world. Identity here is a collective cultural experience.

Next, I explore the ideas of classification and value as a way of thinking about social identities. The chapter follows with a discussion on the

The woman in pieces   81

relationship between advertising, totemism, and consumption, showing how ads trigger a classification system that is central to modern life. Then, I present a brief explanation about method and the Brazilian political context of the 1980s that point to some important ideas to understand the feminine identity projected by ads of that decade. Finally, I investigate the meanings that women's images in advertising construct, showing the fragmentation of the female body as a mechanism for promoting products and services in Brazil. As we are going to see, the fragmentation of the female body in advertising is a strategy that creates possibilities, spaces, and markets for different brands to position themselves as owners of each one of the pieces, establishing specific territories for their various consumer goods.

2 Identity, classification, and value

Ideas like identity, person, character, mask, or role can be related to the debate over performance or acting in everyday life. These are terms that refer to traditional sociological subjects – interaction, groups, power, social organizations, and so on – and involve several complex theories of the Social Sciences. Nonetheless, the concept of social role is one of the ideas that most come up when discussing society. The concept appears in familiar expressions, such as "role model," "play a role," or "have a role in," as much as in formal discourses that define the attributes and functions of proper roles. Similarly, the idea of "status" rather close to the idea of role enjoys some popularity, and both deserve an in-depth study, a true archaeology of the structures and contexts by which different authors have considered them.

A study on these two concepts would certainly refer to theater as a metaphor. In Ralph Daherendorf's famous book *Homo Sociologicus*, a classic on the investigation of social roles, the theater theme is clearly presented:

> Role, person, character, and mask are words that, despite being originated from different stages of linguistic development, share a common area of meaning: the theatre. In drama, for example, we speak of people or characters whose roles are played by the actor. Although currently, in general, the actor no longer uses the mask, this word too has the same origin.[2]
>
> (Dahrendorf, 1964/1969, p. 43)

The theater metaphor is also found in Goffman's "dramaturgical perspective." In an interesting scheme described in *The Presentation of Self in Everyday Life*, Goffman (1959) explains that the "self" acts projecting his characters toward characters projected by other "selves" that are the audience as well. A third word from the theater, the audience is in everyday life formed by those who watch the performance of the "self." All that is explained in the preface, where the author emphasizes the importance of

82 Perspectives on consumption (media images)

the theater metaphor: "The perspective employed in this report is that of the theatrical performance; the principles derived are dramaturgical ones" (Goffman, 1959).

Dahrendorf's use of the idea of theater in *Homo Sociologicus* is clear as well. The text opens with the idea of *theatrum mundi* as one of the first metaphors used in this sense. The human world is like an immense theatrical drama and all living individuals play a single role. Next, Dahrendorf quotes the famous line of Shakespeare's character Jacques in the comedy *As You Like It* as an example of a new view on social role. Jacques says, "All the world's a stage and all the men and women merely players." In this view, there is not a single role for each human being, but roles that succeed each other in time, one after another, "His acts being seven ages" in a sequence that ends only with death. The point is that each different age described in Shakespeare's play is also related to professional roles, such as student, soldier, and judge. Each professional role, in a certain sense, defines an individual in a proper age to occupy it (Dahrendorf, 1964/1969, p. 47).

From the perspective on human life as a single role – *theatrum mundi* – then as a sequence of roles during a lifetime – "His acts being seven ages" – we finally come to the idea of multiple and nonexclusive roles that each of us is supposed to play. According to that last perspective, individuals may undertake multiple roles and activate each one of them in different moments. A great deal of the social role debate converges toward that idea. Dahrendorf (1964/1969) creates a famous example of a situation where a certain Dr. Hans Schmidt, unknown till this moment, is introduced in a meeting. Once better acquainted and after gathering information about him, we come to acknowledge that there is only one Hans Schmidt, although he is engaged in many different positions and social roles: adult, man, married, citizen of German nationality, father, professor, and so on. This example shows that the individual's indissolubility is a notion implicit in social identity. Dahrendorf (1964/1969) explains the *homo sociologicus* as the tension and the intersection between the individual and the social. Individuals are constituted by their preestablished roles, but these are also the boundaries that society imposes on them.

Hence, identities and social roles are at the crossroads between individuality on the one hand and society on the other. It is difficult to dissolve the category of "individual" and examine it as a social construction. Such a fundamental category in our culture is often perceived as an absolute truth, inalienable, independent, and beyond every concrete social or historical experience. This reification and universalization of the individual is the path followed by part of the discussion on social identity. Ethnocentric views transform the idea of the "individual" into something absolute. The Brazilian anthropologist Roberto DaMatta (1983) observes:

> One could say that, for English Anthropology, the practice of the discipline seems to pose a kind of contradiction: if, on one side, there is a

The woman in pieces 83

search to fulfill a collective or holistic perspective, there is, on the other side, a need to forever recover the "individual" that is, in fact, an irreducible value of its own system.

(p. 44)

Roberto DaMatta criticizes a few of Edmund Leach's studies about social organization that, like others in English anthropology, tend to see society as the result of assembled trajectories, transactions, and individual strategies. Depicted like this, social life comes out as reference, invention, and result of an unceasing negotiation of private and individual interests. But if we think of the "individual" and "individualism" as concepts related to our ideology rather than to the nature of identity, we may move forward to a less sociocentric perspective from where we can start thinking about social identities.

The individual should be understood as a social category. Not all societies transform the individual into a substance so relevant to their existence. In Western culture, the individual is the center of the system, a kind of yardstick to many attitudes and thoughts before the world, and constitutes an inner space, an isolated unit opposite to the social system. The individual has choice, feelings, and the authorship of our intimate novel. The individual makes many of the rules of the world it inhabits. However, the individual is also an ideological construction of certain social systems. Its empirical and physical reality is no assurance that every culture will turn it into a social value. As DaMatta explains (1979):

On one plan, we have the empirically given notion of the individual as a concrete, natural and inevitable reality, independent of collective and individual ideologies and representations. Thus, we know that there is no human social formation without the individual. But, between acknowledging the empirical existence of the individual and taking it as a relevant and active social unit in a social formation, capable of generating the coexisting ideals of individualism and egalitarianism, there is a social and historical fact, a product of the development of a specific social formation: Western civilization.

(p. 171)

There is a distance between the empirical reality of the discontinuity of bodies and individualism as an ideological creation of a given society. That distance is enough to avoid a general and absolute understanding of social identity based on the reification of the individual. So, if we consider the individual in a relativistic perspective, how should we think over the matter of identities? Dahrendorf offers an alternative by placing the concept of social role at the intersection between individual and society. Though his terms – individual and society – seem to agree with the sociocentric viewpoint that DaMatta mentions, his idea that identity happens in an intersection

84 *Perspectives on consumption (media images)*

is interesting. In other words, I propose that identity is located at a cross-roads, but one that is free of preestablished contents. Identity needs a place, but that place does not need to be where the categories of individual and society intersect. If the individual is socially and historically constructed value of a "specific social structure," it cannot be at the same time one of the axes that define identity in every culture. As something elaborated by a given culture, Western civilization, the individual is parallel and not paired to society, which makes any intersection impossible. Nonetheless, the idea of thinking the concept of social identity as an intersection between two axes opens a path for a relativistic point of view as long as these axes bear no content specific to a particular society. Two plans may cross, but instead of individual and society, I propose classification and value.

This "geometric" metaphor serves as an exercise to support another perspective for understanding social identities. Like so many anthropological themes, the notion of social identity requires a fine-tuning between ideas sufficiently abstract to resist ethnographic diversity and precise enough to interpret concrete social experience. The reflection concerning social identity is a paradox, because it must presume the particularity of every culture and, then again, the existence of the phenomenon in multiple cultures. Because of that paradox, the issue of social identity requires an open interpretation, like the ideas of classification and value that result in specific forms of choice and realization of concrete identities once intersected in any context. Classification and value are means of construction, operation, and distribution of social identities. Through them, it is possible to walk away from the ethnocentric entrapment and avoid the Western individual as explanation for the notion of identity in all societies.

Classification is a place in the structure that must be filled so the world becomes coherent and intelligible to social actors. Lévi-Strauss's work (1962a, 1962b) shows that the necessary coherence to wholeness means to allow multiple translations among its parts; however, these parts may permanently serve as means to recover wholeness. Every combination establishes different meanings or values, which are spaces filled with content by the position the classification system itself defines. Thus, classification indicates a specific position while value gives meaning to this position in the structure. This pair, classification and value, enables one to understand how in a given social system local conditions define a set of local identities. In this sense, classification and value are ways of creatively dealing with the particular and the universal in social identities. Next, I propose to test these ideas in advertising, making explicit its classificatory vocation and looking at the values the media attributes to feminine identity.

3 Ads, totemic systems, and consumption

According to Lévi-Strauss's teachings (1962b) in *La Pensée Sauvage*, classification is an exhaustive process. Through classification, culture inscribes

The woman in pieces   85

its particularities in the world. Nothing would make sense if we did not obtain meaning from everything that surrounds us. The process of classification establishes order, difference, and meaning. Existence assumes a human atmosphere, everything acquires a place, because to us it is impossible to live in inconsistency: "(...) 'you can't have all the world a jelly' (...)" (Douglas, 1966/2003, p. 38).

Lévi-Strauss showed that the phenomenon known in anthropology as "totemism" is, in fact, a taxonomic scheme that establishes homologies between two separate domains. Totemism classifies things by using differences in the natural sphere to create differences within the cultural sphere. The totemic type of classification is how certain societies make their world coherent through the mutual translation between nature and culture. By harmonizing these two opposite spheres, societies interpret and transform "their" world into an integrated space. But to find coherence in connecting nature with culture, totemic logic has to make time cyclic instead of linear, to bet on structure and its maintenance, suspending the passing of historical time. Differently, modern Western societies, which privilege linearity and change in their readings of the world, often refuse classification systems like "totemism" that are machines for the suppression of time (Lévi-Strauss, 1962b).

Even in modern Western societies, however, there are openings, ruptures, and contradictions that create spaces where classification systems similar to totemism operate. I consider that advertising is one such space. Ads routinely transmitted to us play a drama that emulates life, but removes from it pain, misery, anguish, doubt, and human frailties. The world it portrays is just perfect. In ads, products have feelings, there is no death, and happiness is absolute. Children smile, women desire, men are fulfilled, and oldness beatifies. Ads show a world that is neither truthful nor misleading: it is magical. In advertising, like in myths, we follow narratives where animals speak and magical events repeat themselves. Ads edit the reality of everyday life to produce idealized narratives. In the "society of reason" remains a tacit commitment to believing in the impossible.

Advertising classifies and hierarchizes *The World of Goods* (Douglas & Isherwood, 1979), engendering relationships not just among goods but among people as well in the arena of consumption. The manifest function of ads is to sell products and services, but a closer look shows that to some extent, goods are what audiences least consume. Every ad sells lifestyles, feelings, and worldviews in generously larger portions than cars, clothes, or toys. Products and services aim possible buyers, but advertising messages are distributed indistinctively, an aspect that favors their classificatory character. Advertising speaks of the eternal, suppresses historical time, converts differences in the series of production into differences in the series of consumption. That is, advertising performs the function of mediating the opposition between the two central domains of capitalist economy: production and consumption. Ads reimagine products, giving them

86   *Perspectives on consumption (media images)*

an identity, specifying and preparing them to exist outside the mechanical sphere of production and imbedded in symbolic and social relations of the humanized sphere of consumption.

Production and consumption are complementary but substantially different processes. Production is marked by inanimate materials, machines, serialization, and anonymity. Products are multiple and impersonal. In the sphere of production, humans are absent and alienated from their work (Marx, 1867/1977). However, products that are impersonal, serialized, and anonymous must be consumed by human beings, introduced in discontinued social segments, incorporated in spheres of singularity. They must have a face, a name, and a story to occupy a place in the symbolic order.

To introduce the outputs of production in the sphere of consumption, advertising and marketing have to omit the social history of products and reencounter humanness in the symbolic order. In the bourgeois world, consumption is the arena of difference. Products and services are one of the central elements in the construction of our identities, worldviews, and lifestyles. Nothing is consumed in a neutral way. Consumption translates a universe of distinctions: the symbolism attached to products and services allows them to fulfill their classificatory vocation. The advertising system attributes names, contents, representations, and meanings to a constant flow of goods. Many would not even make sense if a label did not offer them the proper classificatory information.

Advertising classifies products, gives meanings to services, positions goods, and creates hierarchies of objects. This system draws a map of needs and reasons, writes a script of feelings that attaches contents to types of products, turning them from homogenous things into specific brands endowed with names, places, and purposes. Thus, advertising is an instrument of selection and categorization of the world that creates nuances and particularities in the mechanical domain of production and reciprocally differentiates groups, situations, and moods in the humanized domain of consumption.

The classification principle that operates in advertising opens a path for studying the issue of social identity through its vast repertoire of images. Specifically, in this chapter, I investigate the contents that ads select to ascribe to representations of women. But to understand social identity, there is also the axis of value. Classification defines a space; the next step is to investigate the values that fill it. Here, I study ads that, through the goods or themes they display, seek to classify women's universe and to attribute values to their images in a process that constructs a model of feminine identity.

4 Brazilian society in the 1980s: notes on method

This work examines magazine ads published from 1980 through 1989, with the purpose to reveal advertising representations of women in the Brazilian society of that decade. In order to investigate media discourses that

The woman in pieces   87

refer to the female universe, I submitted a collection of standard one-page ads to a textual analysis (Bauer & Gaskell, 2000; Titscher et al., 2000; Duarte & Barros, 2009). Both the visual and the written dimensions of advertisements were considered in this investigation, aiming to identify some of the main characteristics of women's media images of that time. Hence, the analysis reflects on the syncretism between visual and verbal languages, which are basic aspects of every ad in print. In effect, ads published in magazines of weekly or monthly distribution adequately conjugate verbal and visual expressions to materialize abstract contents and fulfill its commercial purpose.

I selected ads from five Brazilian magazines – *Nova, Claudia, Playboy, Isto É*, and *Veja* – which were among leading periodicals in the national market of that decade. The material compiled was separated into 21 classes, according to the type of product or service announced. This typology is a "native" process of classifying ads used in the professional world of advertising to establish categories in its innumerous contests and prizes. In a previous work (Rocha, 2010), I adopted the same criteria to analyze the "liquor" class. Now, I chose the categories of "cosmetics and toilette" and "clothing and textiles." The first category includes ads for creams, lipstick, lotions, perfumes, powders, bathing salts, dentifrices, deodorants, soaps, shampoos, depilatories, sprays, hair dye, nail polish, brush and comb in general, tanners, sanitary pads, and shaving razors and related items. The second comprises ads for clothing in general; lingerie; textiles; wools; leather goods; shoes; bed, bath and table linen; and sports apparels. Both categories were selected because ads for these types of products were mainly directed to women.

The collection of magazines searched includes 1,400 editions from 1980 through 1989. In the 1980s, an average issue had about 100 pages. Each edition had almost 50% of its pages dedicated to one-page ads. The estimated universe is 70,000 ads, which were divided considering the 21 categories mentioned above. Evidently, some categories have more products and services advertised than others. But on average, we can estimate there is something like 3,300 ads for each category. For this analysis, two categories were chosen: "cosmetics and toilette" and "clothing and textiles." Considering that in these categories about 20% of advertisements are directed to the male readership, there were 5,280 ads available for examination. Nearly 5% of them (260 ads) offer us a significant material for analysis, because they emphasize women's bodies, sensuality, and beauty. From that selection, I present here some of the advertisements for the following brands: *Max Factor, Chique, Appel, Del Rio, DeMillus, DuLoren, Lib Slip, Matitte, McChad, Sulfabril, U.S. Top, Helena Rubinstein, Hidraskin, Skin Dew, Wella, Sanny, Power Bust Flex*, and *Dropnyl*.

Another important thing that gives consistency to this textual analysis and that may offer us some clues to understand the image of women is a description of the Brazilian historical context in the 1980s. This should help

88   *Perspectives on consumption (media images)*

us to understand the ideological patterns that emerge from women's representations in ads, which are directly related to cultural models, political behavior, economic reality, and social life as experienced in the great Brazilian urban centers of that time. In fact, the 1980s in Brazil were characterized as a crucial moment of passage from a military dictatorship, which began in March 1964, to a desired re-democratization. This transition was gradual, slowly conquered, but still a sustained process that began in the late 1970s and was fulfilled with the presidential election in 1989, the first one to happen by popular vote in almost 30 years.

In 1960, Brazilian voters democratically elected president Jânio Quadros for a five-year mandate. However, the president suddenly resigned from his post in less than a year and was replaced by Vice President João Goulart. This was a period of political turmoil with changes from a presidential system to parliamentarism and then back to the presidential model again. In an ideologically complicated and tense setting, a military *coup d'état* happened in March 31, 1964 (Dreifuss, 1980). This military regime ruled the country for the next 20 years, alternating five generals in the presidency and maintaining a submissive National Congress that was powerless to question military decisions. The dictatorship created its own laws, censored the media, violently persecuted adversaries of the regime, and destroyed organized political groups and parties. The remaining professional politicians, by personal interest or by lack of options, accepted the military terms and were divided into the only two parties that were permitted: MDB and Arena (Gaspari, 2002a). A private Brazilian joke of that time said that the country had two parties: one that said "yes" (MDB) and the other that said "yes, sir" (Arena) to military orders.

The dictatorship reached its most radical moment between the end of the 1960s and the first half of the 1970s with the publication of the "institutional acts" establishing nondemocratic changes in the Constitution. This is the moment in which the country experienced the greatest repression in the cultural and political levels in recent history. No newspaper, radio, television, or magazine could publish anything without going through previous censorship. The cultural production – of books, films, plays, visual arts, dance, and even soap operas – was heavily censored (Gaspari, 2002b). Because of this terrible climate of cultural oppression, it became almost mandatory for the media, including advertising, to use patriotic elements and support the so-called "Brazilian economic miracle" in its narratives. In fact, the main local client of advertising agencies at the time was the government that commissioned self-promotion campaigns to elevate its accomplishments and ideology. However, in the second half of the 1970s, economic crisis and changes in the international political scenario led to an increase of popular dissatisfaction that forced the military to begin a process of opening the regime, including the amnesty of political exiles in 1979. Ads selected for the present study were published during the 1980s, a period of increasing political and cultural flexibility, which included

The woman in pieces 89

elections for state government by popular vote and the election of a civil president by the National Congress (Gaspari, 2003).

For the purpose of this study, this is a crucial period, because besides incipient possibilities of once again establishing democratic political practices, other social forces also repressed by the regime started to find spaces for their manifestations. This is the case of the feminist movement and the growing presence of women in Brazilian social, cultural, and political life (Costa & Sardenberg, 2002). In 1980, for example, *Rede Globo*, the most important Brazilian network since that time and currently among the biggest of the world, launched two television shows that placed women's everyday problems and possibilities as central issues of debate. One of them was a primetime fictional series called *Malu Mulher* that approached themes like female work, male oppression, sexual abuse, relationship problems, and so on. The other one was a variety show called *TV Mulher* that touched on conservative topics like culinary and decoration, but also bold ones such as freedom of speech, job market, the female body, and intimacy. Incidentally, the strong sexuality of films such as *Fatal Attraction* (USA, 1987), in which a man is threatened by the obsessive desire of a woman, was a subject of exciting conversations in social gatherings in Rio de Janeiro. This was also a time when many women singers, such as Rita Lee, Maria Bethânia, Simone, Joana, Fafá de Belém, among others, became big stars of the Brazilian music scene with songs that expressed the female point of view about love, relationships, desire, and so forth (Fernandes, 1987; Xavier, 2007; Mattos, 2010; Ribeiro, Sacramento & Roxo, 2010). In universities and Brazilian scientific associations of the Social Sciences, women's studies, feminism, and gender-related issues began to appear as respectable objects of academic debates, supported by scholarships and research grants. In 1981, the Brazilian government sanctioned the UN convention of 1967 about the elimination of every form of discrimination against women. Also, during the 1980s, the number of women working in government and private companies began to increase (Miceli, 1995; Costa & Sardenberg, 2002).

As expected, this complex process of political and cultural re-democratization of the 1980s in Brazil is marked by an increase in popular demands that were long repressed. The feminine universe reproduces this exact atmosphere of breaking limits and creating possibilities. For women, the beginning of public discussions concerning their insertion in society as professionals, their sexuality, maternity dilemmas, and political participation combined multiple kinds of needs and expectations. This summary of the re-democratization period in Brazil gives an idea of the cultural circumstances behind female representations in the 1980s advertising. Therefore, ads analyzed in this chapter express their connection with their time, constructing the woman's image as an individual with uncertain possibilities in a body that is exposed in multiple fragments and desires of consumption.

90 *Perspectives on consumption (media images)*

5 The body in pieces: the fragmentation of women

The designated place in the classification system and its hierarchical position indicate a space to be filled with values that build the feminine identity. In examining ads, the first thing that calls attention is that women are classified in relation to men and also several types of the female gender. The "woman" is different from the notions of "girl" or "young lady." In an ad for *Max Factor*, for instance, an exuberant woman's picture and a sentence define the difference: "Some things are just better in a woman than in a girl." The advertising system shapes the woman's identity in opposition to the masculine universe as well as the idea of "girl." Her place may even be the same as that of a "thing" as a text for "Del Rio" lingerie, which accompanies photos of women, significantly without a face, suggests:

> Many beautiful and well-made things fit in a soft *Lycra* set by *Del Rio*: the *Lycra* bands and more resistant seam, the bra's shaped pad, the panty's anti-allergic cotton interior, the charming backstitch, needle or lacework, and you, another pretty and very well-made little thing.

Similar to a "thing," different from a "girl" or subordinate to "men," women's identity finds a space between contrasts that is covered up with values. A fundamental value that articulates all others is the idea of individual that ads attribute to feminine identity. The need to ascertain women are not just "human beings" but "individuals" as well appears very clearly in a text that promotes *Nova* magazine to advertising agencies: "*Nova* is the magazine of women as human beings. *Nova* is not the family magazine nor the home magazine or the children's magazine. It's the magazine of women as individuals." The notion of individual or of individuality is a marked value in the construction of women's identity. For example, an ad for *Chique* perfume states: "There are many ways you can be yourself. But none of them are quite that chic." The notion also appears in the following ads for *Matitte* and *DuLoren*:

> *Matitte* is the jeans label that respects all your gestures, your expressions and your individuality. Wherever you are, it is the pair of jeans that complements your will to come and go freely. No censures, no inhibitions. Involve yourself with *Matitte* jeans.
>
> This summer, be a woman even underwater. Wear a *DuLoren* bathing suit. And leap. Leap into the sun, into the sea or in the swimming pool. Leap in fashion. With the new *DuLoren* submarine collection you are much more of a woman, inside or out of the water.

The ideas of "you being yourself," the respect to "individuality," and "be a woman even underwater" show the first mark advertisements establish in feminine identity. It seems so necessary to claim the woman is "herself,"

The woman in pieces 91

has a "self," and shows "authenticity" as if an obvious collective value – the individual – needs to be explicitly connected to the women too. To build or to reinforce the individual as value is a fundamental advertising operation. Ads must emphasize buying as an act of will, commanded by rules of choice that has the individual at the center. Accordingly, terms like "want," "desire," "choice," "will," "freedom," and so on are often used with eloquence in advertising narratives. These are generic ideas that can be used for selling dresses to women as much as for selling cars to men. So far, the analysis suggests that ads for men and women can be quite similar. Regardless of the identity at stake in representations and images, the desire to reinforce the individual as a central value is present. Advertisements define consumption as an arena of individual choices and imply it is a "natural" act, something in the sphere of free will that happens in the subjective decision plan as an assertion and exercise of singularity. In this sense, ads only synthesize a key operation of the broader phenomenon of consumption.

However, ads do not seem to reinforce the relationship between male "individuality" and consumer goods as much as they emphasize the connection of female "individuality" to products and services. This difference becomes clearer when investigating values that are specifically distributed delineate female individuality. The individual as a "woman" turns into a "body" whose possession, use, beauty, treatment, and enhancement are at stake. Ads establish the body is a property, a fundamental good and value of this individuality, a territory of feminine action. For example, an ad for *Artemis* expresses this idea in a short line: "*Artemis* [is] the best in your body." Another ad for *DeMillus* is more emphatic; after the title "Put your body in the right places," a text compares the idea of individuality to the woman's body:

> Women need to position their bodies in relation to life: they need to come out with presence, stirring up love fires. To do so, they must always be in the right places, letting nothing escape from all a woman has to offer. With *DeMillus* shapers, you put your body in the right places.

The body as main possession, the very translation of the "woman" individual is recurrent in several ads. But what is significant in many of them, different from others that speak of the whole body, is the focus in different and fragmented body parts. An ad for *McChad* jeans serves as an example of this approach. While its image focuses on the "waste," "buttocks," and "thighs," the text says, "Brazilian anatomy. Few jeans manufacturers understand the lyrics of this samba." Another one refers only to the "buttock" and, along with a meaningful picture, gives women an order to "Enhance the filling of *Lib Slip* – the disposable panty." This body in pieces may be depicted also as just "breasts":

> How to keep your breasts firm and stiff? Forget all you have ever seen about miraculous balsams, creams and ointments to tighten your

92 *Perspectives on consumption (media images)*

breasts. There is only one organic and natural way to accomplish this: strengthening the pectoral muscles. And there is only one way to strengthen them: making specific exercise, like *Power Bust Flex.*

The body's fragmentation continues in representations of women's "face" that, in the following ads for *Helena Rubinstein* products, appears prominently in photo and text:

> The power of pastels. The summer makeup. Gentle tones, but vibrant at the same time... created specially to enhance your face in the irresistible fashion of pastel colors.
>
> At last, there is a compact eye shadow that lasts longer. Have a firm and uniform coloring, in a delicate movement, with the new applier that is adjusted to your eyes' natural curves.

There are many possibilities for advertising to translate feminine individuality as the property of a body and its parts. And advertisements indefinitely fragment the body, breaking it up in as many pieces as necessary for the product – hair, feet, hands, nails, eyes, eyelashes, legs, breasts, buttocks, teeth, skin, among others. In this dismantled body, one part stands out for its constant need of treatment. The skin, according to ads, is always somewhat "sick" or "damaged" and in need of "treatment":

> *Hidraskin.* It's the simplest and most efficient way to treat your skin. Whatever your skin type, the new *Hidraskin* line is the complete care you need. Do your beauty treatment with *Hidraskin* and have a healthy, soft and very, very pretty skin.
>
> After creating the makeup, *Max Factor* creates the beauty treatment within the makeup. Whipped cream makeup collection, the makeup treatment. You make yourself up. You treat your skin. Now, you have a makeup line so rich in moisturizers that act as a beauty treatment while you are with your makeup on.

The quite "indecipherable" universe of the "skin" and by definition its permanent "lack of treatment" is a chapter apart that deserves an entire study. And no matter the skin, because "if you have normal or dry skin, *Skin Dew* is the most complete and efficient treatment line you can find." In this very particular fragment of the body, notions such as health, treatment, depth, moisturizing, humidifying, dry, beauty, natural oils, and others repeat themselves, creating a world that can be unknown and dangerous if not properly protected by products. A careful study of advertising texts for "skin" products gives interesting material to discuss the things this mysterious "dermatological" world in ads is capable of. Inevitably, this reminds me of the Barthes's (1957/1997) comments concerning advertising's very peculiar appropriation of the idea of depth:

The woman in pieces   93

All advertising of beauty products is similarly based on a kind of epic representation of the intimate. The little scientific prefaces, meant to introduce (and to advertise) the product, ordain that it cleans in depth, relieves in depth and feeds in profundity, in short, at any price, it infiltrates. Paradoxically, it is insofar as the skin is first of all a surface, but a living, hence a mortal surface, likely to dry out and to age, that it readily assumes its role as a tributary of deep roots, of what certain products call the *basic layer of renewal.*

(p. 47)

However, the body's representation goes beyond the pure and simple possession of its parts since they must be "embellished," "enhanced," and "accentuated." Seen as the body is the main property, a kind of fundamental exchange good of this "woman individual," it must be more. Like in the example that follows, the body has to be "stretchy" as well:

This fabric's elasticity is the latest thing by *U.S. Top.* It stretches where it needs to: in width. A fabric like this allows a perfect adjustment that appreciates your body and your swing. As for your body's stretchiness, you just have to do a little work out.

The body has to be "elastic," "stretchy," "swingy." The many possibilities translated by images of the feminine body appear as well in ads for a *De-Millus* campaign, through women's expressions in photos and the contents of the following texts:

Free the flower of your body. Your body is a flower. And flowers need freedom to blossom. In light moves, in appearances that fit to moments, its lines must correspond to situations. *DeMillus* gives the liberty you need, with soft, stretchy and gentle bras that allow your body the freedom to show itself.

Feel a touch in your body. The touches in your body should be the right caresses in the right places. *DeMillus* has a nice touch for you to always remember: soft, shapeable, comfortable, a dream of stretchiness. *DeMillus* has the prettiest touch for a woman in this bra detailed with a Richelieu cut that will never let you forget your charms.

The sweetest embrace you can get. An embrace from *DeMillus* is full of emotion: warm, soft, stretchy, modeler, to be remembered forever. *DeMillus* understands a woman's needs and delivers its quality in little sets like this, in striped *Lycra*, that give women's bodies the embrace they need.

Representation of the female body expresses freedom, because its nature is that of a "flower" that wishes to "blossom." Her body must be "caressed," "soft" the way you like it. It must always "remember" the "gentle

94   Perspectives on consumption (media images)

touches," getting "the right caresses in the right places." The body, shaped and bendy, is ready to receive the "sweetest embrace" that must be "full of emotion." Therefore, products "understand a woman's needs" better than anyone else.

The body is marked as a central value of the woman's individuality. Furthermore, it is in many ways fragmented, detailed, and examined. It is divided into parts, and some of them may be "enhanced" while others can be "treated." The body must be "stretchy," "embraced," "caressed," "touched," and... "free". It is a flower, and also permanently in lack of something, needing to be "cared," "embellished," and "accentuated." All this is because the body, while property and basic element of the individual, must be used as the main strength, power, and *locus* of the event of the woman's individuality.

Still, women's images in advertising are more complex. They are submitted to the broader representation of the individual in contemporary culture. And though the representation of the individual is to some extent experimented by the body, its emphasis is on something this body carries as essence, content, or substance. The "individual" results from the combination of body and spirit. Generally, the substance – described in terms like "mind," "soul," "head," "self," "spirit," and so on – has predominance over the material dimension – the body – that sustains it. That is why not even in the magical world of advertisements, the feminine individuality is framed just by the body.

The woman portrayed in ads has to be more. It is up to advertising to balance the dimensions of "substance" and "body," distinguishing them according to gender. "Substance" and its qualities are usually prevalent in masculine identity. However, the "body" and its qualities are prevalent in feminine identity. Nevertheless, as seen before, it is necessary to amass other values in order to make both components of "individuality" compatible as a broad cultural representation. Thus, the woman in ads acquires apparently more "spiritual" contents in the search to recover coherence between terms. For example, in the next ad for *Wella's Kolestral* cream, under the title "A woman with a mind of her own," a text speaks of other values:

> In charge, up to date and ready for life. Every day she accomplishes her own space in order to fulfill her fundamental role in society. This is today's woman that always values her own charm. She never surrenders what she holds as most important: her femininity.

The analysis of ads shows that in line with that notion of feminine "spiritual" values, there are certain ideas that give "content" to this "individual." The woman must be things that refer to and connect with the body. She must be "in charge," "up to date," "ready." Like an ad for *Sanny*, a clothing manufacturer, tells us, products must offer "new intimacy concepts." The "intimate" content that will fill the inner space explains itself in the image of a woman with a provocative look, half-opened mouth, wearing only

The woman in pieces   95

her underwear. Beneath the title "woman in very saucy version," a text suggests that feminine individuality corresponds to certain characteristics: "*Sanny* proposes new intimacy concepts. It is something that has much to do with the new, emancipated, and very sexy woman of our time."

The body's content, therefore, is that of "a new, sexy, emancipated woman of our time." She must express her inner self emphatically. As the following ads state, "I wear *Dropnyl* because I'm beautiful, modern and intelligent" or "I wear *Dropnyl* because I love compliments." Besides affirming the self, an ad for *Sulfabril* shows other contents, because the woman it portrays must "dare to use a *Sulfabril* fabric" and "stick to a promise until the end." Ads conceived the inner space of the feminine individual through referring to and emphasizing an erotic, beautiful, sensual plan that finds, again, in the body its only possible instance of translation.

Nonetheless, this "individual" needs to "speak." And it is from the "substance" or "spirit" that speech is made possible. Since the feminine individuality that advertising projects is mostly sustained by the "body," words will have to be expressed by another instance: the product. Like the ads say, "Find yourself in a DuLoren" or "Win your space by the clothes you wear." In them, products literally take the place of the woman's speech: "Elegance, class and lots of charm. *Appel*: the perfume that speaks for you." When reading the ads below, it is interesting to notice how "she" delegates her ideas and words to products that take charge of the "inner woman" as representatives and expressions of her desires, wants, thoughts, and emotions:

> *Lipmaker*: a luminous idea in your lips. It's mainly with your lips that you show you have brilliant thoughts. That is why *Max Factor* created *Lipmaker*, a lipstick different from everything you've ever seen. Put this word in your mouth: *Lipmaker*.
>
> Make your words last even when conversation is over. *Max Factor* Color Fast Long-Lasting Lipstick. A lipstick that has a formula specifically created to stick more to your lips. With the new Color Fast Lipstick by *Max Factor* you put a colorful and sparkling cream in your lips that lasts as much as the impressive things you say. With Color Fast Lipstick the conversation may end, but never the spark.

Ads construct a version of feminine identity by attributing certain notions and marks to it. First, there is the previously discussed idea of "individual" since it is a fundamental operation of advertising to transform the impersonality of production into the particularity of consumption. The "individual" is emphasized as basis to identity, because consumption must be experimented as a volunteer act, a kind of affirmation of the "self," something in the sphere of private choices. The "woman" portrayed supposes the presence of a consumer individual whose value is reproduced in ads. Therefore, the starting point is to construct representations of women as "individuals" that have the desire for consumption as their core value.

96 Perspectives on consumption (media images)

Second, representations of women in ads have their individuality specifically characterized in the idea that this "woman individual" means primarily the ownership of a "body." However, this "body" is not represented as a "natural" unit. The body is divided into parts and manipulated to become matter capable of being indefinitely fragmented. It is like a mosaic made up of pieces that, if isolated, do not outline a picture and therefore do not signify. This body, dissolved into many fragments, is the main power of the "woman individual" that, through it and almost exclusively by using it, makes herself bold, modern, seductive, in charge, and so on. Broken into multiple pieces, this feminine body prevents the unified construction of a fundamental dimension of individuality, that is, its "substance" – "mind", "spirit", and so on – so the individual can be complete. The representation of a fragmented "body" may indicate that an equally fragmented "substance" corresponds to it. So, individuality does not acquire consistency and the inner plan does not sustain itself.

In this sense, the "woman individual," as shown in advertising, when existing mainly as a fragmented body, makes impossible the construction of an "inner plan" and consequently the realization of speech. The third mark fixed to the feminine identity in ads is that of a silent woman that possesses a body and must know how to use it, even though words are forbidden to her. Since "she" does not own a "substance" or, at least, has it in precarious form, her speech is pushed to another instance. Hence, the "woman" in advertising assigns "words" to products that "speak" for her, reveal her "ideas," and express her inner self as "needs" and "desires." Only they can understand her.

Certainly, a broader study of women's images throughout advertising would include further dimensions not perceived in this exercise. The analysis of other types of products – for children, cleaning, foods, or household appliances – could indicate, for example, the existence of representation of women as "housewives" or "mothers." Advertising studied as a production system of the contemporary collective imagination raises complex questions. This chapter does not presume to exhaust the subject. Its aim was to discuss the problem of social identity as an intersection between the axes of classification and value and through the investigation of ads.

This chapter showed some of the ways advertising frames feminine identity. From the analysis of the "woman" created by ads emerges an image of individuality in which the "body" – and not the "substance" – is what matters. Also, advertising reveals that the feminine body suffers a process of fragmentation through which unity is lost and parts prevail over whole. The woman in ads exists, above all, in pieces – breasts, feet, legs, skin, face, nails, hands, buttocks, eyes, lips, lashes, thighs, and whatever other part that can be detached – as an inverted puzzle with dislocated bits hiding the picture that is never formed. Of course, this image of the body and its pieces cannot sustain the individual as wholeness. Thus, the Western individual, while believing in materiality and substance, transforms itself in

The woman in pieces   97

something twice as uneven. First, the individual becomes uneven because individuality is seen as a relationship between body and spirit, matter and substance, and not only one of these terms. Second, not even the body, which subsists in feminine individuality, is integrated. Like the individual in advertising images of women is undone by the absence of substance, also the matter – the remaining term – is undone by the lack of unity between parts. And then, the "woman" represented in ads silences, since speech is an expression of the "spirit," proper of singularity. What is left of the woman's image is a body or pieces rests fragments of it that without alternative delegate words to products.

The analysis of ads shows that the female body is divided, broken, shattered into multiple fragments in order to serve consumption purposes. A "woman in pieces" appears as an ideological strategy to open new market spaces for products and services that become holders of these evermore specific territories of the body. In the 1980s, amidst the process of Brazilian re-democratization, a moment when new political forces – including feminism – looked to give voice to their demands and to occupy spaces, the woman in advertising images was silenced. The demands for female autonomy and freedom of that time were transformed into mere consumer desires. In fact, ads reveal a woman fragmented into several parts that translate the idea of a perfect female body as the support for a wide variety of consumer goods. At the same time, this body in pieces becomes itself the very object of consumption. Finally, the "woman" constructed by ads lets products take their place as owners of choices, desires, and needs. They "speak" for her, and certainly in advertising representations, the woman must keep herself in silence.

Notes

1 See, for example, Frith, Shaw and Cheng (2005), Bordo (1993), Sneeringer (2004), De Grazia and Furlough (1996), Wiles, Wiles, and Tjernlund (1995), and Kuhn (1985).
2 All quotes from Portuguese editions were translated to English by the author.

References

Banet-Weiser S., & Portwood-Stacer L. (2006). I just want to be me again! Beauty pageants, reality television and post-feminism. *Feminist Theory, 7*(2), 255–272. https://doi.org/10.1177/1464700106064423.
Barthes, R. (1997). *The Eifflel Tower and Other Mythologies* (R. Howard, Trans.). University of California Press. (Original work published 1957).
Bauer, M., & Gaskell, G. (Eds.) (2000). *Qualitative Researching with Text, Image and Sound: A Practical Handbook for Social Research*. Sage.
Bordo, S. (1993). *Unbearable Weight: Feminism, Western Culture, and the Body*. University of California Press.
Costa, A., & Sardenberg, C. (Eds.) (2002). *Feminismo, ciência e tecnologia*. Redor/Neim/UFBA.

98 Perspectives on consumption (media images)

Dahrendorf, R. (1969). *Homo sociologicus* (M. Berger, Trans.). Tempo Brasileiro. (Original work published 1964).

DaMatta, R. (1979). *Carnavais, malandros e heróis*. Zahar.

DaMatta, R. (1983). *Repensando E.R. Leach*. In: R. DaMatta (Ed.), *Edmund Leach* (pp. 7–54). Ática.

De Grazia, V., & Furlough, E. (Eds.) (1996). *The Sex of Things*. University of California Press.

Douglas, M. (2003). *Purity and Danger*. Routledge. (First published 1966).

Douglas, M., & Isherwood, B. (1979). *The World of Goods: Towards an Anthropology of Consumption*. Basic Books.

Dreifuss, R. (1980). *State, Class and the Organic Elite: The Formation of an Entrepreneurial Order in Brazil 1961–1965*. The University of Glasgow.

Duarte, J., & Barros, A. (Eds.) (2009). *Métodos e técnicas de pesquisa em comunicação*. Atlas.

Durkheim, E. (1970). *Sociologia e filosofia* (J. M. de Toledo Camargo, Trans.). Companhia Editora Forense.

Fernandes, I. (1987). *Memória da telenovela brasileira*. Brasiliense.

Friedan, B. (2012). *The Feminine Mystique*. W. W. Norton & Company. (First published 1963).

Frith, K., Shaw, P., & Cheng, H. (2005). The construction of beauty: A cross-cultural analysis of women's magazine advertising. *Journal of Communication*, 55(1), 56–70. https://doi.org/10.1111/j.1460-2466.2005.tb02658.x.

Gaspari, E. (2002a). *A ditadura envergonhada*. Companhia das Letras.

Gaspari, E. (2002b). *A ditadura escancarada*. Companhia das Letras.

Gaspari, E. (2003). *A ditadura derrotada*. Companhia das Letras.

Geertz, C. (1973). *The Interpretation of Cultures*. Basic Books.

Goffman, E. (1959). *The Presentation of Self in Everyday Life*. Doubleday.

Goffman, E. (1977). La ritualization de la féminité. *Actes de la recherché en sciences sociales*, 14, 34–50.

Kates, S. M., & Shaw-Garlock, G. (1999). The ever entangling web: A study of ideologies and discourses in advertising to women. *Journal of Advertising*, 28(2), 33–49. https://doi.org/10.1080/00913367.1999.10673582.

Kilbourne, J. (2000). *Can't Buy My Love: How Advertising Changes the Way We Think and Feel*. Simon & Schuster.

Kuhn, A. (1985). *The Power of the Image: Essay on Representation and Sexuality*. Routledge and Kegan Paul.

Lévi-Strauss, C. (1962a). *Le totémisme aujourd'hui*. PUF.

Lévi-Strauss, C. (1962b). *La pensée sauvage*. Plon.

Lynn, S., Hardin, M., & Walsdorf, K. (2004). Selling (out) the sporting woman: Advertising images in four athletic magazines. *Journal of Sport Management*, 18(4), 335–349. https://doi.org/10.1123/jsm.18.4.335.

Marx, K. (1977). *The Capital: A Critique of Political Economy* (B. Fowkes, Trans.). Vintage Books. (Original work published 1867).

Mattos, S. (2010). *História da televisão brasileira: Uma visão econômica, social e política*. Vozes.

McLuhan, M. (1951). *The Mechanical Bride*. Beacon Press.

McRobbie, A. (2009). *The Aftermath of Feminism: Gender, Culture and Social Change*. Sage.

Miceli, S. (Ed.) (1995). *História das ciências sociais no Brasil*. Sumaré.

The woman in pieces 99

Phillips, E. B. (1976). Novelty without change. *Journal of Communication*, 26(4), 87–92. https://doi.org/10.1111/j.1460-2466.1976.tb01941.x.

Ribeiro, A., Sacramento, I., & Roxo, M. (2010). *História da televisão no Brasil.* Contexto.

Rocha, E. (2006). *Representações do consumo: Estudos sobre a narrativa publicitária.* Mauad and PUC-Rio.

Rocha, E. (2010). *Magia e capitalismo: Um estudo antropológico da publicidade* (4th edition). Brasiliense.

Rocha, E. (2012). *A sociedade do sonho: Comunicação, cultura e consumo* (5th edition). Mauad.

Sneeringer, J. (2004). The shopper as voter: Women, advertising, and politics in post-inflation Germany. *German Studies Review*, 27(3), 477–501. https://doi.org/10.2307/4140979.

Titscher, S., Meyer, M., Wodak, R., & Vetter, E. (Eds.) (2000). *Methods of Text and Discourse Analysis: In Search of Meaning.* Sage Publications.

Wiles, J. A., Wiles, C. R., & Tjernlund, A. (1995). A comparison of gender role portrayals in magazine advertising: The Netherlands, Sweden and the USA. *European Journal of Marketing*, 29(11), 35–49. https://doi.org/10.1108/0309 0569510100696.

Xavier, N. (2007). *Almanaque da telenovela brasileira.* Panda Books.

6 Classified beauty
Goods and bodies in women's magazines

With Marina Frid

1 Brazilian culture and women's images

This chapter investigates how women's magazines in Brazil construct notions of feminine health, beauty, and well-being. Specifically, its contribution is to show that these notions are created through a logic that resembles totemism in order to promote a myriad of consumer goods in society. We will demonstrate this mechanism relating consumption to a totemic type of classification through the analysis of Brazilian magazines – *Claudia*, *Nova*, and *Boa Forma* – that target a female readership. In contemporary life, we seem to be constantly exposed to ever new possibilities of accomplishing and maintaining strong, slim, and forever young bodies, a phenomenon that is translated into a kind of ideological pressure for individuals, especially women, to chase and conform to a model of "perfect shape." From the latest scientific findings – such as medical research, the possible cure of a disease, or a new virus – to beauty treatments and countless methods for slimming, strengthening, and embellishing the body, information about well-being-related issues are good material for magazines. The explicit project of magazines seems to be the offer of a compound of ideas about everything that is new, innovative, and modern, encouraging personal and, as seen particularly in this analysis, bodily changes. However, through a careful and systematic observation of their contents, we may begin to perceive something else: the permanence, the recurrence, and the invariability behind frequently proclaimed ideas such as the "new," the "latest," and the "next" that are the very drivers of the success of magazines. Therefore, this chapter uncovers a magical appropriation of time underlying the ideological commitment that associates consumer goods to never-ending transformations towards an unreachable, desired, and dreamlike shape.

The emphasis of Brazilian women's magazines on aesthetic aspects of bodies and their exhibition reflects certain particularities of a country that has warm weather almost all year round and where many important cities are coastal or very close to the seashore. In Brazilian imaginary, outdoor spaces, especially beaches, have important meanings for sociability as places to see and to be seen, where bodies are in constant display. The cultural

DOI: 10.4324/9781003176794-8

appropriation of the beach was consolidated around the 1920s, related to ideals of cosmopolitanism and European fashion. Particularly, Rio de Janeiro and its beach lifestyle usually emerge in everyday life and media discourses and even in academic studies as a metaphor for the entire country (O'Donnell, 2013). At the beach, different urban groups, no matter their social class, income, or age, share the same space, and in spite of possible tensions, people show and use their bodies while engaging in leisure, sports, or social activities at any time. Thus, magazine representations reproduce and reify a kind of body cult in Brazil (Goldenberg, 2002; Pravaz, 2009) that is connected to the tropical climate, urban conditions, and cultural values.

Women's magazines compile, edit, arrange, and teach the immense repertoire of social meanings and ideals, especially those that concern the body. Therefore, in this chapter, we propose to analyze women's images in magazines, indicating that behind the ceaseless innovations and renovations they portray, there is also a particular form of classification and suppression of linear time that resembles totemism, as established in the anthropological tradition by Lévi-Strauss (1962). According to the author, totemism is a way of understanding reality. Totemism is a form of escaping chaos, an effort to create and attribute meanings that organize living beings and things in social life (Lévi-Strauss, 1962).

Studies explore the presence of women models in the media, the gender and power-related issues in such representations, and the political uses of the feminine image in mass communication through various perspectives and theoretical frameworks (Goffman, 1979; Kuhn, 1985; McRobbie, 1997; Kates & Shaw-Garlock, 1999; Lindner, 2004; Crymble, 2012; Drake & Radford, 2019). A number of authors investigate how mass media appropriates feminist discourses as presenting products and services (Goldman, Heath & Smith, 1991; Banet-Weiser & Portwood-Stacer, 2006; D'Enbeau, 2011), while others look to understand, through different approaches and conceptual backgrounds, the social dimensions of the profusion of goods today and the psychological impacts of idealized images of happiness, beauty, well-being, and the perfect body (Bordo, 1993; Kilbourne, 2000; Dittmar, 2007; Harper & Tiggemann, 2008). Authors also explore and compare beauty ideals constructed in women's magazines, particularly in ads, in countries such as Singapore, Taiwan, South Korea, and the US (Frith, Shaw & Cheng, 2005; Jung & Lee, 2009).

This chapter focuses on the correlations between goods and bodies that sustain a permanent logic of consumption. As we examine here, Brazilian magazines appear to classify an infinite array of products and services according to representations of female body parts. In this sense, we apply Lévi-Strauss's (1962) understanding of totemism to investigate the meanings of magazine narratives and their relation to consumption. Specifically, the analysis points to existing "islands" of permanence despite the ideology of change that media productions express and different authors discuss as a characteristic feature of contemporary cultures, linked to global networks

102   *Perspectives on consumption (media images)*

of consumption, mass communication, and information technologies (Jameson, 1998; Tomlinson, 2007; Lipovetsky, 2009).

To understand the specificity of media representations of the female body in our present material, we begin by referencing studies on Brazilian culture, especially the classical works of Gilberto Freyre (1936/2003) and Roberto DaMatta (1979) and their discussions of the feminine ideal. According to both authors, women embody traditional values, always tied to the domestic space and ruled by the male universe, even if in certain circumstances their image may show otherwise. To them, this means that women in Brazil carry a central ambiguity.

Freyre (1936/2003) observes that the transition from an agrarian-patriarchal society – where women have a passive role in the domestic sphere – to an urban-industrial society in the late nineteenth century did not bring significant changes to their autonomy. Urbanization was an opportunity for women to emancipate themselves from the oppressive power of the pater family through gradually assuming men's functions in the public sphere as they were incorporated into the workforce. This incorporation, however, was not translated into liberty and power but became a double shift because, from then on, women accumulated new professional tasks with old household duties. To DaMatta (1979), the well-known exhibition of Brazilian women at beaches or during Carnival celebrations does not mean general individual liberty or sexual freedom, but a regulated display of their bodies in certain places and times. Carnival is a ritual that inverts the logic of society, shifting routines, combining different socioeconomic levels, and gathering a mass of individuals on the streets regardless of their status, interpersonal relationships, and economic conditions. Carnival is when society's marginalized and oppressed elements may come out to more prominent positions. So, women appearing in a leading role during this festivity represent an inversion of the Brazilian social structure, where the feminine value is encompassed by the male value and, above all, connected to the domestic realm. Recent works through diverse perspectives and contexts analyze women's place in Brazilian culture, further exploring questions in regard to democracy, social hierarchies, racial differences, rituals, stereotypes, beauty ideals, and body shape images (Lewis, 1996; Caldwell, 2000; Labre, 2002; Goldenberg, 2005; Pravaz, 2008, 2009). Although concerned with current aspects of women's place in contemporary Brazilian society, these studies still corroborate to some extent the interpretations of both Freyre (1936/2003) and DaMatta (1979). Work does not mean autonomy and nudity does not mean the right to control her own body. Both can happen, though still under the power of traditional forces.

2   Ambiguity and magazines

An examination of women's images in three examples of Brazilian advertising for over two centuries sustains the ambiguity that classical studies refer

Classified beauty   103

to. Modeling the female body according to a specific standard of beauty has been a permanent ideology for almost 150 years. Despite women's accomplishments, they are still subject to a form of control exerted over their bodies, as we can see in three ads from 1875, 1980, and 2013 that repeat the same pattern. Ever since the late nineteenth century, an ad suggested a corset that could press a woman's body without oppressing her flexibility was the magical solution:

> What lady, who is indeed a bit covetous of keeping her waist in elegant proportions, will not let herself be seduced by these delicate corsets Cintura Regent and these elegant shapes from Escoffon house, (...), which have improved even beyond the impossible? (...) it preserves your waist without making you squeeze into a tight corset; it presses your belly without oppressing your flexibility.
> (Freyre, 1936/2003, p. 220)[1]

The perfect corset could model the female silhouette according to the late nineteenth-century dominant pattern, making her waist overly thin without however taking away all of her freedom. As seen in Chapter 5, an ad from the 1980s for a body shaper, which is a contemporary version of old corsets, seems rigorously equivalent to the one from 1875 in its promise to shape the feminine body:

> Women need to position their bodies in relation to life: they need to come out with presence, stirring up love fires. To do so, they must always be in the right places, letting nothing escape from all a woman has to offer. With *DeMillus* shapers, you put your body in the right places.

Like her earlier version from the late nineteenth century, the woman in the advertising campaign for *DeMillus* needs to put her body in the right places. So on the one hand, her individuality is in the possession of a body. On the other hand, she is still subject to a form of power translated into consumer goods that aim to adjust her silhouette according to an ideal of feminine beauty. An ad for an anti-cellulite pantyhose, another type of underwear that models the female body, published in July 2013 in *Claudia*, continues to perpetuate a similar message:

> Every woman has her mysteries. Comfortable and discreet, *Sigvaris Sculptor* is the anti-cellulite pantyhose that reduces undesirable dimpling and models an attractive silhouette. You just need to slip on the pantyhose to immediately begin your treatment. *Sigvaris Sculptor* makes you more beautiful, more confident, and happier.

As the ads indicate, the ambiguity persists in Brazilian culture for at least 150 years. On the one hand, a woman "without oppressed flexibility,"

104 *Perspectives on consumption (media images)*

"with presence," "more confident and happier" is supposedly free and in control of her own body. On the other hand, she is compelled to fulfill dominant social patterns with "elegant proportions," a body that shows "all a woman has to offer" and an "attractive silhouette." These three examples illustrate how the modeling of women's bodies according to specific products is an old and well-established sales and advertising strategy. In the remainder of this chapter, we will further examine this pattern that connects women's bodies, body parts, and personality traits to the specific benefits of products.

Images of feminine bodies used for commercial purposes in mass media carry complex cultural meanings in Brazil and elsewhere (McLuhan, 1951; Barthes, 1957; Goffman, 1979; De Grazia & Furlough, 1996). It is precisely the complexity of meanings involved in representations of the female body that our analysis of women's magazines, *Claudia, Nova*, and *Boa Forma*, collected from August 2011 through July 2013, will look to understand. In order to investigate magazine materials that refer to women's body shape, health, and appearance, contents – especially news, stories, and articles – are subject here to a textual analysis (Titscher et al., 2000). As Barber (2007) indicates, texts are reflexive; they are both produced by and interpretations of society, offering "(...) a unique insight into their own operations as acts of cultural instauration" (Barber, 2007, p. 5). For her, written texts, as other oral, performance, or object compositions, should be regarded not just as "windows" that may give access to something else, but as the very terrain of investigation. Hence, both the visual and the written dimensions of contents were considered in this study, aiming to identify some of the cultural meanings that encompass women portrayed in these Brazilian media productions.

Boa Forma (Portuguese for "good shape") is entirely dedicated to beauty, health, and body care themes, while *Claudia* and *Nova* (Portuguese for "new") approach a variety of subjects such as relationships, career, fashion, family, house decoration, culinary, and travel. In fact, these were the leading publications for women in Brazil till the mid-2010s.[2] For an overall idea of the contents, missions, and editorial projects of these magazines, it is interesting to observe how they presented themselves to potential advertisers in 2014.

With over 50 years in publishing, *Claudia* entitles itself as the "maximum authority"[3] when it comes to indicating possibilities for women in pursuit of a "better version" of themselves. The reader of *Claudia* is independent and enjoys taking care of herself as much as "she likes to bond her family and celebrate friendship." *Nova*, which was the Brazilian version of North American *Cosmopolitan*, stimulates and guides women in "chasing their career goals, attracting their life partners and standing up for their choices." The magazine inspires "boldness," encouraging women to face challenges and seek "pleasure without guilt." Finally, *Boa Forma* helps women to become prettier "from head to toe," and its readers are always

Classified beauty 105

ready to "change their attitudes toward life and to promote transformations in a healthy and responsible way."

During a period of 24 months, from August 2011 to July 2013, these magazines were collected and examined in order to perceive some of the representations of women's well-being, beauty, and fitness currently displayed in Brazilian imagination. Many interesting observations about the ideological place of women can emerge from the reading of each edition. However, magazines reveal more once perceived as a structured group, according to the textual analysis. This way, we are able to notice the recurrence, invariances, and permanencies behind multiple images and texts that are always intending to offer updated, fresh, and last-minute information.

According to statistics we consulted in 2014, the monthly amount of readers of *Claudia* reached 1,775,165,[4] *Boa Forma* 1,159,548,[5] and *Nova* 695,121.[6] So, magazines were estimated to reach millions of individuals throughout the country. On average, *Claudia* has about 230, *Nova* 170, and *Boa Forma* 130 pages per issue, totalizing almost 6,500 pages per year, since these magazines were distributed on a monthly basis.[7] Advertisements, strictly speaking, represent around 50% of every edition, not counting all indications of products and services that are found in almost every story. Hence, this chapter results from an analysis of a material comprising 74 editions and about 13,000 pages.

The purpose here is to show a system of classification and a cyclic temporality that resembles the logic of totemism in the persistent connection of body-consumer goods in magazine covers, columns, and stories. We examine 26 covers of *Boa Forma*, the section "*Saúde*" ("Health") from every issue of *Claudia*, and two stories "*Porção Sexy*" ("Sexy Portion") and "*Tiro ao Alvo*" ("Target Shot") published in *Nova* in November 2011 and March 2012, respectively. *Boa Forma* is entirely committed to topics related to health, well-being, and body care; therefore, we analyzed its covers, which is the most important and expressive part of any magazine. *Claudia* brings an extensive variety of themes, reason why we chose to focus specifically on the "Health" section, which is dedicated to the body. *Nova* publishes as well diverse subjects and the selected stories called our attention for explicitly connecting parts of the body to specific consumer goods. The analysis of these materials indicates there is room for permanencies behind the profusion of ever new media representations. In this sense, this study finds a contradictory immutability in magazines' discourses of novelty and change.

3 Linear perspective and totemic systems

According to modern belief, rationality, scientism, political laicism, and the related reduction of the importance of magic are responsible for human development from savageness to the enlightenment. In fact, this conception of humankind in progressive evolution from a "primitive," weak, and unprotected state is particular to Western culture, as "(...) we are the only

106 *Perspectives on consumption (media images)*

people who think themselves risen from savages; everyone else believes they descend from gods" (Sahlins, 1976, p. 53).

Lévi-Strauss (1962) shows that any culture is in fact capable of disinterested thinking, even if its intellectual concerns do not aim the same questions of modern science. "Savage thought" is different because it wishes to achieve an absolute understanding of the world, starting from the premise that everything has to offer sense or else nothing makes sense. Conversely, in the name of scientific progress and industrial development, modern culture sought to establish a rational form of objective thinking that allows the creation of a never-ending chain of inquiries about humans, nature, and its elements. In this diachronic perspective, the result of a project is always destined to become the proposition that inspires the following. But the mythical or magical thinking associated to supposedly "primitive" cultures is synchronic, elaborating structures through rearranging facts or reminiscences of facts that are all-embracing and already available as means for reflection. Hence, if scientific thinking looks to change the world creating facts through structures, magical thinking creates structures through facts (Lévi-Strauss, 1962).

Magical thinking obtains continuity through a classification system that creates differences from homologies between nature and culture. If culture is the human domain while nature is the "nonhuman" territory, the purpose of this system known as "totemism" is to conjugate elements of the natural sphere with elements of the cultural sphere. Totemic systems give sense to the world through connecting social groups or clans to animals, plants, and other things they define as natural. For example, the Chickasaw – a tribal society of the Southeastern Woodlands in the US, studied by ethnologist John R. Swanton in the 1910s and the 1920s (Swanton, 1928/2006) – understand diseases as the result of conflicts between humans, animals, and vegetables. On one side, "angry" animals can cause humans to fall sick; on the other side, vegetables are humans' allies and offer them treatments. This means that animals and vegetables correspond, respectively, to specific human diseases and remedies. So, stomach aches and leg aches are related to snakes, vomits to dogs, jaw pains to deer, belly aches to bears, dysentery to skunks, nose bleeds to squirrels, jaundice to otters, lower abdominal and bladder disturbances to moles, cramps to eagles, eye illnesses and sleepiness to owls, joint pain to rattlesnakes, and so on (Swanton, 1928/2006; Lévi-Strauss, 1962, p. 217).

Totemism opens the possibility to recover continuity between nature and society through creating differences within a series of social groups that correspond to differences within a series of natural elements. This classification process produces a meaningful structure through establishing complementary relationships between pairs of opposites. Differently, modern culture understands itself through a logic where elements should always derive from previous ones and succeed each other in a linear plan. This form of perceiving reality in a sequential order, with changes that extend through time, constitutes the dominant diachronic perspective of modernity.

Classified beauty 107

Societies that adopt totemism possess a cyclic conception of temporality, that is, past and present are like two sides of the same coin. Magic-totemic systems bet on the structure, refute change, and dismantle linearity. In this sense, no matter how many terms the universe has to offer, they have to be incorporated to a totality, to take part on the classification scheme, and thus fulfill their purpose of maintaining cultural coherence. If our society is devoted to change and to expanding the effects of linearity, there are, in fact, other societies devoted to ignoring change and to expanding the effects of permanency.

Hence, the work of Lévi-Strauss (1962) presents us with two distinct forms of interpreting and experiencing the universe: totemism is predominant in so-called "primitive" cultures, while science is the preferred path of modernity. The first form of thinking operation he calls "bricolage," the second "engineering" (Lévi-Strauss, 1962, p. 26). However, these logics do not necessarily exclude each other, since "bricolage" and "engineering" operations are equally available to humanity.

Lévi-Strauss (1962) himself was inclined to consider that totemic systems of classification were present mostly in tribal groups and absent from the "great civilizations," which privilege science and history as means of understanding. However, mass media – and more specifically, advertising – has been noted as a form of magic in modern-contemporary culture by diverse authors. For instance, Raymond Williams since the 1960s perceived advertising as a magic system. To him, the allure of advertising would be in "(…) a highly organized and professional system of magical inducements and satisfactions, (…) rather strangely coexistent with a highly developed scientific technology" (Williams, 2004, p. 221). Rocha (2010) analyzes advertising as a significant form of totemism in effect today that has the basic reason of reconciling production, which holds certain resemblance with nature as a "nonhuman" territory, and consumption. Production is a domain where human beings are absent, alienated from their work, substituted by machines that create serialized, anonymous, and impersonal objects (Marx, 1867/1977). However, production needs to fulfill the purpose of consumption in order to sustain the capitalist system. Therefore, products – undistinguishable, impersonal, and detached from meaning to consumers – need to acquire a face, a name, and a story to occupy a place in the symbolic order. In a world that "things" are made in industrial scale, advertising becomes fundamental for socializing production, converting lifeless matter into "needs," "utilities," and "desires" (Rocha, 2010).

Thus, the question of totemism could be seen in contemporary Western culture as a process that happens with the purpose to transcend differences between production and consumption. Advertising confers identities, situations, emotions, and lifestyles to products that are at first indistinct, neutral, and serialized, classifying every available element as a consumer good that should occupy a specific position in the symbolic structure. Like totemism, the purpose of this process is the possibility of permanently

108 *Perspectives on consumption (media images)*

recovering wholeness and harmony from any one of the terms that integrate a given order. Both systems – totemism and advertising – trigger the mechanism of complementarity, creating alliances between two opposite domains: nature and culture, production and consumption. Following this path of thought, we will proceed to the investigation of Brazilian women's body images, looking to demonstrate a form of totemic logic present in contemporary magazines.

4 Myths and magical calendars

The traditional totemism studied by Lévi-Strauss (1962) indicates that in tribal societies, an alliance between two opposite domains – nature and culture – sustains the system. The definition of "nature," as he points out, varies from society to society, and every culture may ultimately have its own way of conceiving "nature." Therefore, the idea of "nature" is not an absolute essence or universal. Nature is a cultural concept.

In the case of narratives of the sample withdrawn from magazines, "nature" is conceived as a domain that includes both the human body and certain kinds of consumer goods. To fix the body as a "natural" element is a particular perspective that magazines reveal. For a long time, Social Sciences literature established that the body is an element that has its limitations and potentialities – sides (Hertz, 1909), techniques of uses (Mauss, 1935/1973), flexibility (Mead & MacGregor, 1951), tactility (Montagu, 1971), odors and olfaction (Corbin, 1982), expressivity (Le Breton, 1997) – molded and defined by culture. Also, goods that magazines define as "natural" are, in fact, cultural, no matter what qualities (organic, pure, wholegrain), origins (farm, garden, industry), or names may suggest. This means that "natural" yogurts, juices, or oils, as part of the ensemble of social practices of shopping and consumption, are actually elements of culture.

If both – body and goods – can be considered part of "nature", where magazines placed them or part of "culture," as indicated above, what is the actual opposition that sustains the classification system in magazines? As the analysis will show, the opposition that magazines operate is constructed through a process which creates a homology between a series of differences among body territories and a series of differences among consumer goods.

Nova (ed. 464) instructs women about the main causes of accumulated fat and indicates means to eliminate this problem according to each female body part. In the story called "Target Shot," the magazine says that while sweets are "villains" against a flat tummy, "natural" yogurt can act as a "guided missile" attacking fat in this particular body part. Painkillers, beers, soft drinks, and other beverages cause fatty thighs, but cinnamon serves as the appropriate remedy. "Cherry" is indicated against "cellulites," "olive oil" is good for shrinking up the "waist," "onion" for reducing fat in the "back," and "vinegar" for slimming "breasts." The story indicates foods and drinks that can or cannot be consumed with the purpose of making thinner and

Classified beauty   109

healthier the female body and its parts. Foods and drinks correspond to particular body fragments and are divided between those that exert negative and those that exert positive actions over these specific territories.

The positive and negative effects that magazines confer to these elements and that connect them to women's bodies are described in Table 6.1. This is an example of a totemic logic where the magazine articulates a series of differences between body territories to a series of differences between consumer goods. So, the distinction between "breasts" and "tummy" corresponds to the distinction between "vinegar" and "natural yogurt." At this point, consumer goods target body parts according to their positive effects in reducing or negative effects in accumulating fat.

Another example drawn from the story called "Sexy Portion" can show the increase of complexity of totemic systems presented in magazines. In this case, the homology between the series of distinctions in the human body and the series of distinctions in consumer goods is not just a conversion in terms of positive or negative effects related to fat. Table 6.2 shows, in fact, connections between the human body and consumer goods, but now in terms of magical effects over body territories, such as "skin like baby," "amazing hair," "stronger muscles," "acne extermination," and so forth.

As we can see in Table 6.2, an ordinary fruit in Brazil such as papaya and a not so common vegetable such as artichoke are translated into improvements for women's different body pieces. According to this totemic logic, differences between consumer goods – types of fish, fruits, and vegetables – correspond to differences between skin, hair, muscles, and so on. For instance, in magazines, "cashews" are distinguished from "yellow peppers" as "baby skin" can be distinguished from an "amazing hair." These examples of totemic classification allow for an unlimited fragmentation of female anatomy and reciprocally enable countless consumption practices.

The images of the body like diseases constitute a third example drawn from the "Health" sections of *Claudia* magazines. Following a pattern analogous to the totemic system of disease and healing of the Chickasaw,

Table 6.1 Totemic system based on the story "Target Shot" in *Nova* (ed. 464)

Body part	Magazine	Consumer good
Tummy	Negative	Sweets
Thighs	Negative	Painkillers
Thighs	Negative	Beer
Thighs	Negative	Soft drinks
Tummy	Positive	Natural yogurt
Thighs	Positive	Cinnamon
Cellulites	Positive	Cherry
Waist	Positive	Olive oil
Back	Positive	Onion
Breasts	Positive	Vinegar

110 *Perspectives on consumption (media images)*

Table 6.2 Totemic system based on the story "Sexy Portion" in *Nova* (ed. 461)

Body part	Magazine	Consumer good
Skin	Like baby	Cashew
Hair	Amazing	Yellow pepper
Weight	Lower	Coconut oil
Appearance	Rejuvenate	Kiwi
Cellulites	Eliminate	Red grapes
Skin	Tanned	Papaya
Acne	Exterminate	Pumpkin seeds
Sleep	Well	Cherry
Muscles	Stronger	Codfish
Tummy	Flat	Artichoke

Table 6.3 Totemic system based on the "Health" sections of *Claudia* magazines (eds. 599–622)

Body disease	Magazine	Consumer good
Mood swings	Cause	Margarine
	Antidote	Salmon
Diabetes	Cause	Diet sodas
	Antidote	Apple vinegar
Cancer	Cause	Artificial dyes
	Antidote	Probiotics
Obesity	Cause	Fast food
	Antidote	Liraglutide
Memory loss	Cause	Liquor
	Antidote	Brazilian nut
Heart attack	Cause	Cigarette
	Antidote	Gym

where "angry" animals cause human diseases and vegetables are "allies" in the correct treatment, to readers of *Claudia*, some consumer goods can cause body disorders while others can provide the exact antidote. As described in Table 6.3, "angry" diet sodas can cause diabetes, but an "ally," apple vinegar, can act as a remedy. "Angry" liquor and cigarettes can cause, respectively, memory loss and heart attack, while Brazilian nut and gym are the sacred "allies" that can treat and even prevent these bodily conditions. The classification system indicating a relationship between body diseases or healings and differences among consumer goods may go on indefinitely. In this sense, the totemic system of magazines, like the Chickasaw's, is always inclusive of any disease, their enemies and allies, connecting every existing element and leaving nothing out, as shown in Table 6.3.

Another important feature of totemic systems that is also presented in magazines is the "suppression of time." Mythical-totemic systems are like

Classified beauty 111

machines for the suppression of time, encompassing every natural and social element available in a closed system where the classification process only stops when it is no longer possible to oppose (Lévi-Strauss, 1962). Totemic time – cyclic, recurrent, which bets on permanence and which is parted from the linear order – is a form of temporality that remains implicitly in contemporary societies. This can be most easily observed in rituals such as Christmas Day, anniversaries, Mother's Day, Carnival, Valentine's Day that are characterized for repeating themselves and all their values cyclically. The analysis of the sample material, particularly *Boa Forma* covers, concretely shows how propositions, projects, and desires for weight loss operate within a logic that suppresses time typical of totemic systems.

Weight loss is a central appeal to sell magazines. *Claudia, Nova*, and *Boa Forma* offer countless methods, tricks, diets, and recommendations to "flatten" tummies, "shrink" waists, "burn" fat, "lose" some kilos, and "shape" women's bodies. *Boa Forma* explicitly represents this thin beauty ideal through each and every one of its covers that reaffirm, month after month, the notion that women are in constant need to drop a few kilos, covering an entire year with imperious diets, regimes, and body improvements. *Boa Forma* offers in each one of its editions the latest trends, tips, findings, diets, methods, products and services for improved fitness, well-being, and beauty. If reading covers linearly as they are published, each one appears to promise a new, different, and better way for women to lose weight. However, once gathered up as a group, magazines reveal something else: the same recurrent, persistent, and cyclic movement of losing weight proper of totemic temporality.

Hence, according to *Boa Forma* covers, every month women have the chance to get thinner within a few weeks or even days by adhering to the current diet. As we can see in Table 6.4, headlines for every edition from August 2011 to July 2013 are always persuading women to the idea of losing weight in whatever way possible. If covers are seen separately, magazine diets appear to be logical and rational, relating the loss of certain number of kilos, in a historical amount of time, to the specific use of products and services. If seen together, they repeat themselves in a timeless weight loss project that expresses a "magical calendar." In this sense, magazines reveal a totemic system where every new product and service is reintegrated to the same old body (the reader's body) that must lose, once again, a certain amount of weight as indicated in each and every cover. To follow a linear sequence means to drop a given number of kilos that will accumulate month after month. The bizarre paradox is that any average Brazilian woman of 62 kg[8] that attempted to rigorously pursue magazine goals in this diachronic progression could lose up to 115 kg in two years. Thus, linear time must be suspended, because it is a logical impossibility to experience diets historically.

Evidently, the reading and eventual uses of magazine recipes for weight loss must be experienced in a timeless and synchronic sense, in a way that

Table 6.4 The magical calendar based on *Boa Forma* covers (eds. 295–320)

August 2011	*September 2011*	*October 2011*
Flat tummy: –4 kg in 15 days: 'dry out' diet, five new exercises, creams that speed up the result	Accelerate your metabolism and lose 4 kg in 17 days	Melt 10 kg, design your body, and you can win one out of four cruise trips
November 2011	*December 2011*	*January 2012*
Lose 2 kg in four days with the juice diet, 3 kg in nine days with the gluten-free diet, and 4 kg in 15 days with the lactose-free diet	–2 kg in 10 days switching your lunch meal for a diet shake (no need to give up happy hour)/lose 4 kg right now with the new "weightwatchers" diet	–4 kg in two weeks with the coconut oil diet
February 2012	*March 2012*	*April 2012*
Flat belly diet: –5 kg in one month, plus nine super-powerful foods	Lose 3 kg in 15 days with the miracle noodle diet	Mate tea helps you lose weight! Science proves it. Just follow the diet and lose 6 kg in one month
May 2012	*June 2012*	*July 2012*
Skinny by Saturday! –3 kg in seven days with the detox diet	–5 kg in one month with the flat belly diet	Lose 7 kg in 14 days with the new protein diet
August 2012	*September 2012*	*October 2012*
Flat tummy: –4 kg in a month: 'burn fat' menu and Muay Thai express class	Anti-cellulite kit: –3 kg in 15 days: antioxidant diet that dries out and softens your buttocks, super-effective creams and treatments, self-massage to boost results	Summer challenge: –10 kg and a new body by December (and win one out of four cruise trips!)
November 2012	*December 2012*	*January 2013*
–3 kg in 15 days with the chia diet –2 kg in five days with the detox diet	Thin by New Year's Eve: –5 kg in 15 days with the Dukan diet	Fiber diet. Dry out –3 kg in 15 days
February 2013	*March 2013*	*April 2013*
New natural pills to lose weight, anti-inflammatory diet, melts 5 kg in one month	–6 kg in a month with slim protein diet; our reporter melted 25 kg!	Dry out 4 kg and reduce swelling with the green juice diet
May 2013	*June 2013*	*July 2013*
Lose those last 3 kg with the "burn fat" diet	Save $ and lose 4 kg with the basic food basket diet	–2 kg in seven days with the detox soup diet

seems closer to magic-totemic systems than to the linear perspective. There-fore, the reading must be of a ritual logic in which weight loss does not really seem to be the point, because what should matter is that women buy maga-zines and consumer goods. Weight loss is only possible if associated to cer-tain products or services, as examples withdrawn from covers show: exercises and creams (08/11), cruise trips (10/11, 10/12), juices, gluten- and lactose-free products (11/11), diet shakes and "weightwatchers" diet (12/11), coconut oil (01/12), super-powerful foods (02/12), noodles (03/12), tea (04/12), protein products (07/12, 03/13), Muay Thai classes (08/12), antioxidant products and super-effective creams (09/12), chia seed (11/12), the Dukan and the de-tox methods (12/12), fiber products (01/13), natural pills (02/13), green juice (05/13), basic food basket (06/13), soup (07/13). Magazine covers express a totemic time – cyclic and recurrent – as they suppress linearity, encompassing every new product and service in a permanent desire for losing weight.

5 Consumption and representations of women's bodies

The analysis finds the existence of a totemic system in Brazilian wom-en's magazines and how it establishes relations between body territories and consumer goods. These systems enable an understanding of the logic behind the construction of certain images of women forever looking for beauty, thinness, well-being, and youth. The sample withdrawn from *Clau-dia*, *Nova*, and *Boa Forma* indicates that magazines operate oppositions and complementarities through repeating the same magic classification of goods and bodies. If repetition and constancy are central mechanisms of a formulaic model that sustains different versions of magazines (Narunsky-Laden, 2007), this study concretely shows that recurrence contributes to consolidate a magical thinking structure.

Here, we were able to identify in Brazilian women's magazines charac-teristics of totemic systems – the suppression of linear time, fragmentation/ all-embracement and complementarity/opposition – that open perspectives for future studies. Magazines articulate fat, beauty, and diseases of a body fragmented into territories to a series of differences and complementarities among products and services. Our analysis of "Target shot" and "Sexy portion" stories shows how *Nova* establishes these relationships in terms of more or less accumulation of fat (Table 6.1) and magical transforma-tive effects (Table 6.2). Additionally, *Claudia*'s sections on health not only harmonize women's bodies with certain kinds of goods, but also create an opposition between those that are "allies" and those that are "enemies" (Table 6.3). Finally, we demonstrate through *Boa Forma* covers how the process of associating women's bodies to specific dieting methods and goals elaborates a cyclic calendar (Table 6.4). As the analysis of our sample in-dicates, consumer goods and body fragments are repeatedly differentiated only to be reincorporated to a totality – the woman's image – where every element makes sense according to reciprocal relationships.

114 *Perspectives on consumption (media images)*

Like the traditional totemism that operates a mechanism of similarities and differentiations between nature and culture, stories and columns perform the same process with body parts and consumer goods. This operation can happen strictly in terms of accumulating or eliminating fat, like in "Target Shot"; in terms of magical aesthetic effects in specific body territories like in "Sexy Portion" and in "Health" sections in terms of physical diseases and cures. Also, as established by Lévi-Strauss (1962), magical-totemic systems are machines for suppressing time; it is either the present or the eternal. This same mechanism of suspending time and persistently repeating the same myths was observed through 26 issues of magazine covers. In them, the eternal myth of losing weight returns obsessively in each and every present occasion. Totemic time – in a sense permanent, always recurrent, defiant of the linear order – is the form of temporality that remains implicitly in Brazilian women's magazines.

If the basic purpose of totemism is to oppose and harmonize elements of parallel series (Lévi-Strauss, 1962; Leach, 1970), it seems reasonable to consider that the classification pattern operating in magazine narratives not only links consumer goods to body parts, but creates diversities and similarities that classify women according to an idealized typology. Future studies may reflect on the degree to which the presence of a kind of totemic system in magazines, ads, and other media can establish social differentiations, creating distinct feminine groups in terms of their choices, habits, styles, and practices of consumption.

According to the analysis, magazines copiously offer instructions for women to attain or improve their health, beauty, and well-being, creating multiple differences between regions of her body with the purpose of supporting countless products and services. Even though magazines express ideas of individuation, independence, and liberation, the portrayal of women's bodies obeys a framework of traditional cultural forces. The demonstration of the existence of a kind of totemic pattern in women's magazines also indicates the magical character behind scientific, medical, aesthetic, and hygienic notions that permeate supposedly technical narratives.

As seen in this chapter, the significance of products and services derives from their particular position and relationship with female body parts in a classification system. Thus, magazine narratives can be read in two levels. At the explicit level of representations, magazines express novelty, promoting everything that is advanced, innovative, and up to date for the "contemporary" and independent woman that has choice and power. At the implicit level, however, there is a recurrent pattern of classification that follows a logic that serves the purpose of sustaining a system of consumption. On the one hand, she is autonomous, strong, and unique; on the other, she is dependent and fragmented into pieces that are always receptive to consumer goods, no matter what is offered. What really matter are the constant and multiple possibilities of associating products and services to female body fragments. If the commercial project of magazines is to open new consumption possibilities and transform women into thinner, healthier, or prettier versions of themselves, our investigation finds that this project relies on a totemic classification system to continuously differentiate female body pieces according to consumer goods: juices, yogurts, diets, beverages, creams, medications, therapies, surgical procedures, exercises, and so on.

Finally, the gap between the biomedical reality of women and idealized magazine representations has to be everlasting. In fact, magazines cannot actually carry the task of transforming "real" bodies because, after all, they sustain themselves in the tension between reality and the dreamlike shape. If magazines were to succeed in the purpose of making women achieve their idealized images, they would lose their meaning and reason to exist. To keep this tension steady and permanent, magazines need to turn to totemic systems, using their classificatory vocation as a form of promoting recurrence, stability, and the suppression of linearity. Brazilian women's magazines create always-unreachable body images for readers that should pursue this ideal forever translated into consumer goods. The paradox this study finds is that this project materializes a logical structure that bets on magical thinking and suppresses historical time in the midst of a narrative – magazine narratives – self-defined as always new, advanced, and innovative.

Notes

1 The authors translated all quotes extracted from Portuguese editions.
2 In 2018, *Abril* press went through major changes in its control and structure, which culminated with the end of *Nova* in all platforms. *Boa Forma* was transformed into a website. *Claudia* is one of the very few titles that remain in all platforms, including print.
3 All quotes in this paragraph reflect the official discourse and self-definition of magazines, http://www.publiabril.com.br/, visited on May 28, 2014.
4 "Projeção Brasil de Leitores Consolidado 2012" (Brazilian Estimated Readers 2012), www.publiabril.com.br, visited on 09/06/2014.
5 "Projeção Brasil de Leitores Consolidado 2013" (Brazilian Estimated Readers 2013), www.publiabril.com.br, visited on 09/06/2014.
6 "Projeção Brasil de Leitores Consolidado 2013" (Brazilian Estimated Readers 2013), www.publiabril.com.br, visited on 09/06/2014.
7 *Boa Forma* published two additional editions in December 2011 and December 2012.
8 The average weight of adult Brazilian women (18 years old or more) is around 62 kg, according to IBGE (Brazilian Institute of Geography and Statistics), www.ibge.com.br.

References

Banet-Weiser S., & Portwood-Stacer L. (2006). I just want to be me again! Beauty pageants, reality television and post-feminism. *Feminist Theory*, 7(2), 255–272. https://doi.org/10.1177/1464700106064423.

116   Perspectives on consumption (media images)

Barber, K. (2007). *The Anthropology of Texts, Persons and Publics*. Cambridge University Press.

Barthes, R. (1957). *Mythologies*. Éditions du Seuil.

Bordo, S. (1993). *Unbearable Weight: Feminism, Western Culture, and the Body*. University of California Press.

Caldwell, K. L. (2000). Fronteiras da diferença: raça e mulher no Brasil. *Revista estudos feministas*, 8(2). https://doi.org/10.1590/%25x.

Corbin, A. (1982). *Le miasme et la jonquille: L'odorat et l'imaginaire social, XVIIIe-XIXe siècles*. Flammarion.

Crymble, S. B. (2012). Contradiction sells: Feminine complexity and gender identity dissonance in magazine advertising. *Journal of Communication Inquiry*, 36(1), 62–84. https://doi.org/10.1177/0196859911429195.

D'Enbeau, S. (2011). Sex, feminism, and advertising: The politics of advertising feminism in a competitive marketplace. *Journal of Communication Inquiry*, 35(1), 53–69. https://doi.org/10.1177/0196859910385457.

DaMatta R (1979). *Carnavais, malandros e heróis: Para uma sociologia do dilema brasileiro*. Zahar.

De Grazia, V., & Furlough, E. (Eds.) (1996). *The Sex of Things: Gender and Consumption in Historical Perspective*. University of California Press.

Dittmar, H. (2007). *Consumer Culture, Identity and Well-Being: The Search for the 'Good Life' and the 'Body Perfect'*. Psychology Press.

Drake, C., & Radford, S. K. (2019). Here is a place for you/know your place: Critiquing "biopedagogy" embedded in images of the female body in fitness advertising. *Journal of Consumer Culture*. doi: 10.1177/1469540519876009.

Freyre, G. (2003). *Sobrados e mucambos*. Global. (First published 1936).

Frith, K., Shaw P., & Cheng, H. (2005). The construction of beauty: A cross-cultural analysis of women's magazine advertising. *Journal of Communication*, 55(1), 56–70. https://doi.org/10.1111/j.1460-2466.2005.tb02658.x.

Goffman, E. (1979). *Gender Advertisements*. Harper Torchbooks.

Goldenberg, M. (2002). *Nú & vestido*. Record.

Goldenberg, M. (2005). Gênero e corpo na cultura brasileira. *Psicologia clínica*, 17(2), 65–80.

Goldman R., Heath D. E., & Smith S. L. (1991). Commodity feminism. *Critical Studies in Media Communication*, 8(3), 333–351. https://doi.org/10.1080/15295039109366801.

Harper, B., & Tiggemann, M. (2008). The effect of thin ideal media images on women's self-objectification, mood, and body image. *Sex Roles*, 58(9–10), 649–657. https://doi.org/10.1007/s11199-007-9379-x.

Hertz, R. (1909). La prééminence de la main droite: étude sur la polarité religieuse. *Revue Philosophique*, 68, 553–80.

Jameson, F. (1998). Postmodernism and consumer society. In: F. Jameson (Ed.), *The Cultural Turn: Selected Writings on the Postmodern, 1983–1998* (pp. 1–20). Verso.

Jung, J., & Lee, Y. J. (2009). Cross-cultural examination of women's fashion and beauty magazine advertisements in the United States and South Korea. *Clothing and Textiles Research Journal*, 27(4), 274–286. https://doi.org/10.1177/0887302X08327087.

Kates, S. M., & Shaw-Garlock, G. (1999). The ever entangling web: A study of ideologies and discourses in advertising to women. *Journal of Advertising*, 28(2), 33–49. https://doi.org/10.1080/00913367.1999.10673582.

Kilbourne, J. (2000) *Can't Buy My Love: How Advertising Changes the Way We Think and Feel*. Simon & Schuster.

Kuhn, A. (1985). *The Power of the Image: Essay on Representation and Sexuality*. Routledge.

Labre, M. P. (2002). The Brazilian wax: New hairlessness norm for women? *Journal of Communication Inquiry*, 26(2), 113–132. https://doi.org/10.1177/0196859902026002001.

Leach, E. (1970). *Claude Lévi-Strauss*. Viking.

Le Breton, D. (1997). *Usages culturels du corps*. L'Harmattan.

Lévi-Strauss, C. (1962). *La pensée sauvage*. Plon.

Lewis, C. (1996). Woman, body, space: Rio carnival and the politics of performance. *Gender, Place & Culture: A Journal of Feminist Geography*, 3(1), 23–42. https://doi.org/10.1080/09663699650021927.

Lindner, K. (2004). Images of women in general interest and fashion magazine advertisements from 1955 to 2002. *Sex Roles*, 51(7–8), 409–421. https://doi.org/10.1023/B:SERS.0000049230.86869.4d.

Lipovetsky, G. (2009). *Le bonheur paradoxal: Essai sur la société d'hyperconsommation*. Folio.

Marx, K. (1977). *The Capital: A Critique of Political Economy* (B. Fowkes, Trans.). Vintage Books. (Original work published 1867).

Mauss, M. (1973). Techniques of the body (B. Brewster, Trans.). *Economy and Society*, 2(1), 70–88. (Original work published 1935). https://doi.org/10.1080/03085147300000003.

McLuhan, M. (1951). *The Mechanical Bride: Folklore of the Industrial Man*. Beacon Press.

McRobbie, A. (1997). More! New sexuality in girls' and women's magazines. In: A. McRobbie (Ed.), *Back to Reality? Social Experience and Cultural Studies* (pp. 190–209). Manchester University Press.

Mead, M., & Macgregor, F. C. (1951). *Growth and Culture: A Photographic Study of Balinese Childhood*. G.P. Putnam's Sons.

Montagu, A. (1971). *Touching: The Human Significance of the Skin*. Columbia University Press.

Narunsky-Laden, S. (2007). Consumer magazines in South Africa and Israel, *Journalism Studies*, 8(4), 595–612.

O'Donnell, J. (2013). *A invenção de Copacabana: Culturas urbanas e estilos de vida no Rio*. Zahar.

Pravaz, N. (2008). Hybridity Brazilian style: Samba, carnaval, and the myth of "racial democracy" in Rio de Janeiro. *Identities*, 15, 80–102, https://doi.org/10.1080/10702890701801841.

Pravaz, N. (2009). The tan from Ipanema: Freyre, morenidade, and the cult of the body in Rio de Janeiro. *Canadian Journal of Latin American and Caribbean Studies*, 34(67), 79–104. https://doi.org/10.1080/08263663.2009.10816965.

Rocha, E. (2010). *Magia e capitalismo: Um estudo antropológico da publicidade* (4th edition). Mauad.

118   *Perspectives on consumption (media images)*

Sahlins, M. (1976). *Culture and Practical Reason*. The University of Chicago Press.

Swanton, J. R. (2006). *Chickasaw Society and Religion*. The University of Nebraska Press. (First published 1928).

Titscher, S., Meyer, M., Wodak, R., & Vetter, E. (Eds.) (2000). *Methods of Text and Discourse Analysis: In Search of Meaning*. Sage Publications.

Tomlinson, J. (2007). *The Culture of Speed: The Coming of Immediacy*. Sage Publications.

Williams, R. (2004). Advertising: The magic system. In: A. J. Gedalof, J. Boulter, J. Faflak, & C. Mcfarlane (Eds.), *Cultural Studies: A Popular Culture Reader* (pp. 209–222). Nelson College Indigenous.

7 A star player in the world of goods
Marketing and the first Brazilian soccer celebrity

with William Corbo

1 The game and the goods

In 2020, *Forbes* magazine's annual ranking of the "world's highest-paid celebrities" had three soccer players among the top ten names listed.[1] Cristiano Ronaldo is fourth on the list ($105 million), Lionel Messi fifth ($104 million), and Neymar seventh ($95.5 million). Their high earnings are the result of the salaries they receive from their clubs and the marketing contracts they have with various brands from different industries. Currently, Ronaldo is sponsored by brands such as *Nike, Unilever, Herbalife, MTG, DAZN*, and *Altice*. Messi has deals with *Adidas, Gatorade, Huawei, Mastercard*, and *Pepsi*. Neymar recently signed a contract with Puma, adding another sponsor to a list that today includes *Gillette, Mastercard, Red Bull, TCL, Eletronic Arts, DAZN*, and *Beats Electronics*. This business model that articulates soccer[2] and consumption that transforms star players into advertising notables is practiced around the world at least since Pelé, the "athlete of the century."[3] He starred in dozens of ads and lent his name to products throughout his career and even after retirement. For instance, *Café Pelé* – a coffee brand sold in over 30 countries – is named after him. He was also the face of *Mastercard, Coca-Cola, Nokia, Petrobras, Louis Vuitton*, among other brands. Years before Pelé, however, there was another player who pioneered the combination between soccer and consumption in Brazil. His name was Leônidas da Silva, the player who enchanted the country with his moves in soccer fields and sold all sorts of products in the world of advertising.

In this chapter, we analyze the place occupied by soccer player Leônidas da Silva,[4] known as the Black Diamond, in the advertising market and his impact on consumption patterns in the 1930s and the 1940s Brazil. Our aim is to investigate how, in that context, advertising used soccer to stimulate consumption and, in that process, boosted the sport's popularity as well as the interest and mobilization around it.

Even though he was a Black man in a time of explicit racial discrimination in soccer and in Brazilian society in general, Leônidas was considered a celebrity. The question of Leônidas being a Black player in an environment

DOI: 10.4324/9781003176794-9

120 *Perspectives on consumption (media images)*

rife with racial prejudices, soccer included, was studied, for example, by Gordon (1995), Pereira (2000), Souza (2008), and in Mário Rodrigues Filho's (1947/2010) classic book *O Negro no Futebol Brasileiro*. Here, we emphasize another aspect of Leônidas's professional trajectory: his immense success in advertising and the impact he had on Brazilian culture in general.

Leônidas frequently gave interviews and appeared in news coverage that went far beyond the limits of the sporting press. Newspapers, magazines, and radio programs covered his habits, his humble origins, key events in his career, the controversies in which he was involved, his "brilliant" displays of skill in the field and "decisive" goals. As a celebrity, Leônidas attended shop inaugurations, starred in advertising campaigns, and associated his image and name to diverse brands and products, like watches and cigarettes. Most notably, Brazilian chocolate factory *Lacta* launched *Diamante Negro (Black Diamond)* in his honor in 1938, and the candy bar sells in the local market till this day. Our analysis of media archives aims to explore the construction of Leônidas's public image as the first sports celebrity in Brazil. Through this study, we show a model that articulates soccer and consumption, which was incipient at that time and that continues to permeate contemporary imagination.

As two phenomena central to Brazilian social experience, soccer and consumption involve complex questions and open up a variety of different paths for academic investigation. Each of them configures areas of study in themselves and is the subject of extensive bodies of work. The literature on consumption is more international, while the Brazilian perspective is prevalent among studies about soccer, partly because of the game's local importance. Veblen (1899/2007), Simmel (1904), Sombart (1913/1967), Barthes (1957), Baudrillard (1968/2005, 1970/1998), Douglas and Isherwood (2004), Sahlins (1976), among other classic authors, inspired the expansion of research on consumption and related topics, like fashion and advertising, from cultural approaches (McCracken, 1988; Miller, 1997; Trentmann, 2012, Moeran & Malefyt, 2018). Soccer in the Brazilian context was first discussed by Freyre (1938, 1947/2010). His studies were followed by Guedes (1977), Miceli (1978), Araújo (1980), Rodrigues (1982), and DaMatta (1982, 2006) and more recently by Helal (1997), Toledo (1996, 2000, 2002), Pereira (2000), and Hollanda (2004, 2010). Other authors discuss the sociocultural importance of the sport in different cultures and countries (Duke, 1991; Armstrong & Giulianotti, 1999; Hughson et al., 2017). The works that interest us the most are those that examine the relations between soccer and consumption, whether focusing on the problem of the sport as business (Damo, 2008, 2009, 2012), on specific issues surrounding major sporting events (Damo, 2011; Damo & Oliven, 2014), or on the interactions between the game, mass media, and advertising narratives (Sodré, 1977; Gastaldo, 2002; Amaro & Helal, 2014; Mostato, Amaro & Helal, 2014).

Here, we investigate the association between soccer and consumption in the first half of the twentieth century through the emergence of a business

A star player in the world of goods   121

model that coopted outstanding players for advertising strategies. As a result of that model, players once restricted to the "soccer world" became stars in the "world of goods." Leônidas is emblematic because he was the first soccer player to become a media celebrity in Brazil. He was a local sports idol decades before the emergence of world-famous Pelé. By exploring media records of the 1930s and the 1940s, we can delve into this experience of construction of sports celebrities who are capable of mobilizing crowds and selling all kinds of products and services, and observe the persistence of this model till this day, operating under much the same logical parameters.

We structured our discussion on Leônidas and the relations between soccer and consumption in three parts. In the first part, we explore some of the pivotal moments in the player's career and his consecration as Brazilian soccer's biggest name and idol in the first half of the twentieth century. In the second part, we debate the role of the sporting press and the media in general in the construction of Leônidas's public image as a national hero and a representative of core elements of Brazilian culture. Finally, we turn our attention to analyzing how the soccer player was transformed into a celebrity that attracted huge crowds, influenced social life, and worked actively in the advertising market as an endorser of stores and products as diverse as cigarettes, watches, and chocolate.

As a cultural and collective phenomenon wrapped in symbolism, consumption gives meaning to social life and provides the codes that enable us to comprehend and act in the world in which we live in (Douglas & Isherwood, 1979). Soccer, as social drama (DaMatta, 1982), produces narratives and images of idols and mythical heroes that are central for the sporting press, but occupy a considerable space in the general media as well. This chapter reveals some of the fundamental aspects of the emergence of a model that connects consumption to soccer and that has informed shopping and game experiences to this day. A detailed look at the history of soccer in Brazil shows that players frequently appeared in articles, special reports, and interviews in newspapers, magazines, and radio program since the early decades of the sport's professionalization. Soccer stars of the 1930s and the 1940s generated huge amounts of public interest. Idolized wherever they went, they attracted large crowds and were celebrities with a strong popular appeal. Leônidas was the leading player of his generation despite being a Black man in a context of widespread racism. His controversial attitudes were constantly criticized, but (perhaps because of that) he was the country's biggest sports celebrity in the 1930s and the 1940s, capable of acting in the sphere of consumption and boosting the sales of a range of products (Gordon, 1995).

2 A star in the soccer universe

Born in 1913, Leônidas began to display his soccer skills in São Cristóvão, the old imperial neighborhood in the central zone of Rio de Janeiro, where

122 *Perspectives on consumption (media images)*

he lived for most of his childhood and adolescence. In 1930, before completing the age of 17, he made his debut as a soccer player at Sírio Libanês, a modest club in the nearby neighborhood of Tijuca. Leônidas's former trainer at Sírio, Gentil Cardoso, took him to Bonsucesso club the following year, because the conditions there were better to develop his talent. Despite failing to win the 1931 Rio Championship, Bonsucesso attracted considerable attention for the outstanding performance of its players, finishing in seventh place in a competition that included renowned teams of that time, such as América, Bangu, Botafogo, Flamengo, Fluminense, and Vasco da Gama. At Bonsucesso, playing alongside other Black players who would later become his teammates in the Rio de Janeiro and Brazil national teams, Leônidas's talent was soon evident to supporters and journalists, who boasted about the latest rising star in Brazilian soccer (Pereira, 2000).

The year of 1931 marked "definitively the name of Leônidas in the Brazilian soccer scene. Despite playing for the modest Bonsucesso team, he would soon become known in all soccer pitches in Brazil" (Ribeiro, 2010, p. 36). After outstanding performances in his club and the Brazilian Club Championship title with the Rio de Janeiro team, Leônidas was invited to join the national team for the 1932 Rio Branco Cup along with other emerging talents from Rio. Accompanied in the field by stars like Domingos da Guia, Oscarino, Gradim, and Jarbas, he led the national team in its historical win over Uruguay, scoring both goals in Brazil's 2-1 victory. Winning the 1932 Rio Branco Cup was not just a milestone for the history and self-esteem of Brazilian soccer, but a turning point in Leônidas's career as well. From then on, he was the star player and hero of the national team (Pereira, 2000; Ribeiro, 2010).

The title win generated so much enthusiasm that a jubilant crowd flooded the streets of Rio to welcome the players on their arrival back home. During the celebrations, the players paraded through Rio Branco Avenue in an open truck and felt the warmth of thousands of people deliriously praising them, especially Leônidas and Domingos. From that moment on, as champions of the Rio Branco Cup, the two Black players from Rio became the major stars of Brazilian soccer:

> Domingos and Leônidas, carried by the crowd from the moment they landed, were the most celebrated. Applauded with 'real enthusiasm' by supporters lining the avenue in a display that 'was as powerful as it was spontaneous,' they attracted most of the attention and delirium of the fans. Recognized as legitimate representatives of Brazil, they were greeted, along with the other players, by the head of the provisional government himself, Getúlio Vargas - who, as the delegation passed in front of the Catete palace, remained on the balcony waving to the champions, until the parade was over.
>
> (Pereira, 2000, p. 324)

A star player in the world of goods 123

The success of players like Leônidas and Domingos prompted wealthy Uruguayan soccer clubs to spare no expense in signing them on. While Domingos came to an agreement with Nacional and became the club's idol, Leônidas signed a contract with Peñarol. On December 7, 1932, the newspaper *Jornal dos Sports* reported on Leônidas's words as he embarked to Uruguay: "Through *Jornal dos Sports*, I say my farewell to the people of Rio and the enthusiastic 'fans' who I know I'm going to miss." At the new club, he found it very difficult to adapt. He suffered a series of injuries and his performance failed to match expectations, since "the freedom granted to players in Uruguayan clubs [...] was a problem for Leônidas, who, in order to keep fit in Brazil, had needed to be kept under constant surveillance."[5]

Returning to Brazil in 1934, Leônidas signed with Vasco da Gama, a club that invested in hiring highly successful Black players of that moment, like Fausto – the "Black Marvel" – and later Domingos. Leônidas, however, did not remain in Vasco da Gama for long. Amid political disputes between amateur and professional soccer in Brazil, he decided to sign with the Brazilian Sports Federation (*Confederação Brasileira de Desportos* [CBD]) to play for the national team in the 1934 World Cup in Italy.[6] After a terrible preparation (Pereira, 2000; Ribeiro, 2010), the team was eliminated in the first match after a 1-3 loss to Spain. Scorer of Brazil's only goal, Leônidas managed to stand out amid the disastrous Brazilian campaign and showed glimpses of soccer moves that would enchant the world four years later.

After the World Cup, Leônidas was hired by Botafogo, where he consolidated his status as a soccer star by winning the Rio championship in 1935. After the title, however, the player became involved in public disagreements with Botafogo directors and suffered strong racial discrimination. With the escalation of the controversy, major clubs, directors, and fans declared their opposition to the presence of Black players in their teams (Gordon, 1995; Pereira, 2000; Souza, 2008; Ribeiro, 2010). Unhappy at Botafogo and at war with the club's executive board, Leônidas's contract was sold to Flamengo, which planned to assemble a powerful team for the 1936 season and end an eight-year losing streak in the Rio championship. The arrival of the Black Diamond[7] at Flamengo was welcomed with enthusiasm by the club's already huge fan base, anxious directors, and the extensive press coverage. Amidst all the thrill and expectation, there were also concerns about Leônidas's relationship with coach Flávio Costa, known for being tough on players. At his new club, Leônidas joined former teammates like Jarbas, Fausto, and Alfredinho. In a short while, Flamengo had managed to "reunite Rio de Janeiro's most famous trio of Black players: Domingos, Leônidas and Fausto" (Ribeiro, 2010, p. 101). Over the following years, Leônidas showcased his skills and led Flamengo in memorable games in the Rio Championship, especially against Fluminense, which had a team featuring top players like Hércules, Romeu, Lara, Batatais, Ozorimbo, and Russo (Ribeiro, 2010).

124 *Perspectives on consumption (media images)*

Flamengo's success, Leônidas's talent with the ball, and his increasing fame and social prestige helped foment expectations about the player's performance in the 1938 World Cup in France. This time, the Brazil national team was filled with the country's best players and had carefully prepared for the event to avoid the mistakes that contributed to the disappointing result four years earlier. Brazil started in the competition with a 6-5 win against Poland, a 1-1 tie against Czechoslovakia, and then a 2-1 win over that same team, securing a spot in the semifinals. In the decisive match against Italy, Leônidas was injured and had to stay on the bench, watching his team be defeated by two goals to one. Players and the sporting press vehemently questioned the defeat and blamed referee mistakes for the result (Pereira, 2000; Souza, 2008; Ribeiro, 2010). Disappointed with their elimination, Brazilian players beat Sweden 4-2 in the match for third place. Nevertheless, all expectations concerning Leônidas's performance in the World Cup were exceeded. Emerging as the tournament's top goalscorer and biggest star, he was celebrated as the hero responsible for the Brazilian team's unprecedented and surprising third place. The Black Diamond was hailed as "the best centre forward in the world!"[8] and acclaimed by the entire French press. According to Raymond Thoumazeau, columnist of *Match* magazine, "This rubber man possesses the diabolical gift of being able to control the ball lying down or in the air and shoots explosively when least expected."[9]

Returning from the World Cup, Leônidas was celebrated as the greatest Brazilian soccer player at work (Ribeiro, 2010). In that same year, he won the Brazilian championship with the carioca team. In 1939, he led Flamengo to victory in the Rio Championship. However, his relationship with the club began to crumble the following year. His knee showed signs of strain, and fans became more impatient and mistrustful of their star striker. Despite the criticism, Leônidas scored 30 goals during the 1940 Rio Championship. In 1941, injured and immersed in disputes with Flamengo's directors, the player's contract was suspended by the club. In that same year, Leônidas was convicted for illegalities in his military certificate and spent time in prison in Vila Militar, where he was idolized and admired as the country's top soccer player. After being released, his quarrels with Flamengo worsened and were frequently the subject of news. The press would publish full-page stories, listing all of the directors' complaints about the player's behavior on one side and Leônidas's allegations against the club's executive board on the other (Ribeiro, 2010).

The dispute with Flamengo ended in 1942 when Leônidas transferred to São Paulo, the club for which he would play until the end of his career in 1949. In his debut match against Corinthians, his importance to Brazilian soccer, stardom, and capacity for social mobilization were clear. More than 70,000 people packed the Pacaembu stadium to watch the Black Diamond's first game wearing the São Paulo team shirt, a record attendance in that arena (Ribeiro, 2010). Between 1942 and 1949, Leônidas scored 144 goals

A *star player in the world of goods* 125

for the São Paulo team and won the state championship in 1943, 1945, 1946, 1948, and 1949. At the end of his career, he was still regarded as the best player competing in Brazilian pitches, but was not selected by coach Flávio Costa to join the national team for the 1950 World Cup in Brazil. When the national team lost the championship to Uruguay in the Maracanã stadium, many said that had Leônidas been playing, history would have turned out differently.

3 Leônidas, the media, and visions of paradise

Leônidas's career unfolded in the context of intense political, economic, and cultural transformations in Brazilian society (Pandolfi, 1999; Fausto, 2006). In 1930, the year of his debut as a soccer player, Getúlio Vargas rose to power through a successful revolutionary movement that dismantled the system of power alternation between politicians associated to the cattle ranching elite of the state of Minas Gerais and politicians associated to coffee growers of the state of São Paulo. Because of that power-sharing dynamic, the Old Republic was also jokingly known as the "coffee with milk republic." Vargas remained as president of Brazil for 15 years, oscillating between more democratic and more authoritarian measures until 1945, when the Estado Novo (New State) dictatorship came to an end. During that period, the government implemented a nationalist politics, instituting labor laws, creating State companies, and funding public works. Furthermore, the government worked on modeling and disseminating an ideal of Brazilian identity. In a nutshell, Getúlio Vargas sought to unify the country around a collective project of social development and an ideology that would integrate Brazil's cultural diversity into a single national identity. To achieve its purposes, the State transformed soccer into one of its key platforms for propaganda (Souza, 2008).

The alliance between State and soccer became evident in diverse moments. In 1935, for example, during the clash between clubs, organizations in favor of amateurism and those in favor of professionalism, the federal government intervened to construct a harmonious solution and unify the disparate interests into a common project. In that same year, representatives of the federal government began to follow the development of soccer in the city of Rio de Janeiro closely, setting rules and applying penalties for clubs that breached their contracts with professional players (Pereira, 2000). Again, in 1936, clubs asked the Vargas government to mediate the conflict between them, groups, and associations over the issue of professionalism versus amateurism in Brazilian soccer. These events showed the involvement of the presidency and the broader interest of the State in influencing the paths taken by Brazilian soccer (Pereira, 2000; Souza, 2008).

The transition from amateurism to professionalism was fundamental for the increase in the number of Black soccer players in the clubs and in the Brazilian national team. Regulations introduced to professionalize soccer

126 *Perspectives on consumption (media images)*

were also a way to "dissipate the racial prejudice and discriminations that surrounded players like Leônidas and Gradin" (Pereira, 2000, p. 325). This was an important move to expand the sport's popularity and improve the quality of the show. Moreover, the inclusion of Black players in soccer and their prominence legitimized the notion of Brazil as a nation that values its internal differences. Gordon (1995), however, highlights that the incorporation of Black players in soccer did not end racial discrimination. The main clubs would not allow their Black players, even as paid employees, to visit their social headquarters. However, professionalization did create some space to weaken preconceptions about racial inferiority. The increasing presence of Black players like Leônidas in classic matches between the country's top clubs and in successful performances of the national team contributed to the idealization of a harmonious Brazil, capable of uniting distinct classes and groups around a common project.

In this movement, the sporting press, especially journalist Mário Filho, campaigned hard for the professionalization of the sport and for a greater presence of Black players in Brazilian soccer (Leite Lopes, 1994). While Leônidas was gracing the nation's pitches, the sporting press was expanding at a breathtaking pace and soccer was everywhere in newspapers, radio programs, and everyday conversations in the city. Since the end of the 1920s and the advent of radio, soccer reached an ever wider audience that previously had no access to matches, events, or information about the sport. In the same period, the expansion of the specialized press was also significant. According to research conducted by the National Department of Trade, sports periodicals multiplied from just five titles in 1912 to 58 in 1930 (Souza, 2008). Important publications emerged, like *Jornal dos Sports*, *Rio Sportivo*, and *Mundo Esportivo*. Journalist Mário Filho became a prominent supporter for soccer's development and expansion (Leite Lopes, 1994; Pereira, 2000; Souza, 2008).

In 1931, Roberto Marinho took on the command of newspaper *O Globo* and Mário Filho became head of its sports section. From that point on, the talent of Black players like Leônidas and Domingos was celebrated in the paper's daily coverage and special reports. In 1936, Mário Filho bought *Jornal dos Sports*, founded five years earlier by Argemiro Bulcão. Under his direction, the newspaper began to be printed on pink paper and was transformed into one of the main outlets of the national sporting media. In 1938, together with Roberto Marinho, he launched *O Globo Esportivo*. More than a journalist, Mário Filho became the main disseminator of soccer in Brazil, effusively championing causes that valued the presence of Black players in major clubs and in the national team (Leite Lopes, 1994). For him, these players were the true representatives of the Brazilian soccer style (Rodrigues Filho, 1947/2010). Discussing Mário Filho, Pereira (2000) comments that:

> Since 1931, the journalist already emphasized in the pages of *O Globo* the "bewildering mobility and fast moves" typical of players like Leônidas, acknowledged even by his opponents. Like him, other columnists

A star player in the world of goods 127

in those years were focusing their attention on the emergence, for the first time, of a "characteristically Brazilian technique of extremely quick moves and dazzling improvisation in the most tricky moments" – which distinguished the playing style of Brazilian athletes from the technique and discipline learned from the Europeans.

(p. 331)

For journalists like Mário Filho, Brazilian soccer was seen as "equal in power and art, if not superior, to the soccer played in both Argentina and Uruguay" (Pereira, 2000, p. 331). In this context, the presence of Black players, previously seen as a "shameful deficiency of the sport practiced in the country" (Pereira, 2000, p. 331) became glorified by the press as "the big differentiating factor of Brazilian soccer – helping decisively in the creation of a national playing style" (Pereira, 2000, p. 332). Hence, the sporting journalism of the period, led by Mário Filho, attributed certain moves and characteristics to Black players that would come to be regarded as the specific Brazilian way of playing soccer. In journalistic narratives, idols like Leônidas and Domingos, for example, personified the most important and enchanting features of Brazil's soccer.

Along those lines, Gilberto Freyre's sociology was instrumental in the process of incorporating Black players in the sport while creating an ideal type of "Brazilian soccer." Freyre takes Brazilian society to be marked by a series of economic and cultural paradoxes – European and African cultures, Africans and Amerindians, Jesuits and farmers, masters and slaves, educated and illiterate – that generate tensions, dilemmas, and ambiguities. The specificity of Brazil lies in the attempt to balance these dualities in a positive mixture. The wealth of Brazilian culture would come from the ability to combine oppositions (Araújo, 1994). For Freyre (1933/1975, p. 52): "Nowhere, perhaps, can we observe with equal freedom the encounter, intercommunication, and even harmonious fusion of diverse or even antagonistic cultural traditions as we do in Brazil."

Regarding Brazilian soccer, Freyre emphasizes the contribution of Black participants to the Brazilian way of playing the game, which parted from the stiffer and well-rehearsed style of the British "to turn into a dance full of irrational surprises and Dionysian variations" (Freyre, 1947/2010, p. 25). Domingos da Guia, for example, had added "a bit of samba, a bit of Bahia *molecagem* and even a bit of Pernambuco *capoeira* or Rio *malandragem*" (Freyre, 1947/2010, p. 25),[10] while Leônidas performed a kind of Bahian dance in the field. This image of Brazilian soccer and the depictions of Leônidas in the media can be summarized by Mário Filho's narration of a goal scored in the match against Poland in the 1938 World Cup: "Leônidas is kneeling, tying his bootlace. The Polish goalkeeper takes the goal kick. Leônidas stands up, hits the ball. [It's] Goal for Brazil" (Rodrigues Filho, 1947/2010, p. 218). The representation was one of improvisation, trickery, mischief, and inventiveness in a pure state.

128   *Perspectives on consumption (media images)*

4 A celebrity in the world of goods

Leônidas was the essential reference point in creating and sustaining a fundamental representation of a specifically Brazilian way of playing soccer – inventive, naturally talented, improvised, full of genious heroes and national saviors (Rocha, 2003) – which reinforces a certain desired image of Brazilian culture. Daily news about his performance in the pitch, wearing the shirts of top clubs and the national team, his personal life, injuries, controversies, and agreements shaped the imagination of Brazilians about soccer and, in a broader level, about themselves. With his incisive and constant presence in the media, Leônidas became firmly established as one of the most important celebrities of the 1930s and the 1940s. "Celebrities flaunt whatever a particular society, at a particular moment, values" (França, 2014, p. 25), and soccer is a privileged space for cultures to talk about themselves (DaMatta, 1982). In this sense, the Black Diamond represented a central element of the ideological interpretation of Brazil of that time: the positivity of mixture. As a media representation, Leônidas helped to construct an image of Brazil as a harmonious combination of opposites, capable of overcoming differences and uniting the best of different worlds. This Brazilian image persists even today in advertising narratives and other mass media products, like *telenovelas*, television programs, news stories, and so on (Rocha, 2006).

During his career as a soccer player, between the 1930s and the 1940s, everyone wanted to talk about Leônidas. His popularity and capacity to attract crowds generated countless journalistic stories about his life, habits, and behaviors that went far beyond soccer (Ribeiro, 2010). For example, newspaper *O Globo* published a piece titled "A 'shot' in bachelor life" about Leônidas's wedding, which gathered "numerous admirers of the popular soccer player," including "the president of the club [Flamengo], Mr. Bastos Padilha, and other directors."[11] In another report, we learn the details of the player's childhood in the school he used to study, where he was known as the "teachers' ghost."[12] Indeed, when they needed to sell newspapers and magazines or increase radio audience ratings, all of them talked about Leônidas:

> Journalists relied on Leônidas to fill their pages. 'The Black Diamond visits our offices', visits homes. Wherever the newspaper went, Leônidas went. The fan opened the sports pages and there was Leônidas, smiling at him like an old friend. The fan could cross his legs, recline in the chair, and, without even removing the toothpick from his mouth, have a chat with the inventor of the bicycle kick, totally at home.
>
> (Rodrigues Filho, 1947/2010, p. 214)

Leônidas's fame crossed barriers and surprised even those who had followed his career closely. For journalist Mário Rodrigues Filho (1947/2010,

A star player in the world of goods   129

pp. 194–195), the welcome party for the players who won the 1932 Rio Branco Cup illustrates Leônidas's fame and status as an idol. Though still young at the time, the striker already emerged as the biggest star of Brazilian soccer:

> The CBD joined in with the tributes to Leônidas, everyone just wanted to know about Leônidas and Domingos. One had scored two goals, the other had not let a single ball past. The symbols of Brazilian soccer: Domingos and Leônidas.
>
> There was another: Fausto. But Fausto was faraway, he had not competed in the Rio Branco Cup. So Domingos and Leônidas grabbed all the attention. Especially Leônidas.
>
> During the victory parade, it was impossible to walk down Rio Branco Avenue, it was like the third day of Carnival. Leônidas was on the lowered hood of an automobile, embracing the Rio Branco Cup. 'Leônidas! Leônidas! Leônidas!'

In the 1938 World Cup, Leônidas was the star player of the Brazilian team. The extent of his fame was such that some journalists claimed that "the most famous man in Brazil was Leônidas da Silva, not president Getúlio Vargas" (Ribeiro, 2010, p. 112). On the team's return to the country:

> The Brazilian squad would arrive in a city, the shops would close, and people would swarm into the street to carry Leônidas in triumph. The other players were inside the automobiles, the automobiles drove slowly, at funeral pace, accompanying the Leônidas procession. And everyone thought that they were paying tribute to the Brazilian team. All the players turned up, but the tribute was for Leônidas, just for Leônidas to receive medals, baskets of flowers, club banners, Brazilian flags. The others watched on, squeezed into a room bursting with people, as though they weren't players.
>
> (Rodrigues Filho, 1947/2010, p. 219)

When they arrived in Recife, the Brazilian stars were greeted by a crowd of Pernambuco fans. Amongst the players, Leônidas was the one who received the main tributes. As the newspaper O Globo reported:

> Leônidas, the 'Black Diamond,' who shined in European pitches, was carried in the arms of the people that displayed great enthusiasm and followed the soccer stars to the Grande Hotel. In front of the hotel, a large rally is being held by sporting institutions with the participation of all social classes.[13]

In Rio de Janeiro, fans who went to greet the Black Diamond wanted to touch him, hug him, get his autograph. From the docks to the Botafogo

130 *Perspectives on consumption (media images)*

ground, Leônidas was joined by such a huge and tumultuous crowd that he fainted (Ribeiro, 2010). Even after a few days had passed, the euphoria of the fans did not wane down. More and more people would chase the star, asking for his autograph and making all kinds of requests. What became apparent was that wherever he went, Leônidas drew large crowds, especially "young women." When they passed by the star, they "Stopped, looked at Leônidas, and then carried on their way up and down the avenue, happy as if they had seen a cinema idol" (Rodrigues Filho, 2010, p. 212).

Indeed the idolization of Leônidas was such that the star received a series of prizes. For example, he got a car as a reward for winning first place in a contest sponsored by *Magnólia* cigarettes, the most popular cigarette of that period. Launched in September 1937, the idea behind the contest was to choose Rio de Janeiro's most popular soccer player. To take part, fans had to buy a pack of *Magnólia* cigarettes, write the name of their favorite player on the emptied carton, and send it back to the manufacturer. In the campaign for the prize, Leônidas distributed ballot boxes throughout the city[14] and encouraged people to buy *Magnólia* cigarettes:

> I want to make a suggestion. I think my idea is a good one. I want Flamengo's members and fans to send me just one empty pack of *Magnólia* every week. As you know, the number of Flamengo fans is huge and a pack from each one them, added up in the end, will be enough for my *Chevrolet*. The rest is easy.[15]

Among other schemes, he came up with an unusual idea to boost his chances of victory in the competition: "Leonidas was the star who had the laudable initiative of visiting the Detention Centre to distribute *Magnólia* cigarettes, which friends who did not smoke sent him."[16] Leônidas's popularity was unrivalled and the Flamengo fan base was already the largest in the city. The end result: almost 300,000 cigarette packs had the name of the star, who easily won the competition (Ribeiro, 2010).

With his increasing prestige, Leônidas began to give talks throughout the country in which he talked about the goals scored in the 1938 World Cup and Brazilian soccer in general. The first talk was held in the João Caetano Theatre in Rio de Janeiro. The announcement of the event in *Jornal dos Sports* read: "The 'Black Diamond' will describe to his fans in detail the seven goals that he scored masterfully over the course of the *Coupe du Monde*."[17] *O Globo* reported that "A unique show offered by Leonidas will provide a festive occasion at the João Caetano Theatre tonight to raise funds for the Union of Blind People of Brazil."[18] The newspaper also reported that the second part of the show would feature Ary Barroso, who would be accompanied by other well-known Brazilian musicians and singers, like Benedito Lacerda and Carlos Galhardo. A few days later, the soccer star gave another talk in the city of Belo Horizonte. Actor Procópio Ferreira organized the event and covered all the expenses. Leônidas received half of

A star player in the world of goods   131

the revenue. In the first part of the talk, he read a text written by his friend and journalist José Maria Scassa. Then, he drew all seven goals scored in the World Cup on a blackboard located in the center of the stage. That night, Leônidas wore a tuxedo jacket offered by *Sapataria Capital* as part of a promotional campaign (Ribeiro, 2010).

Like today's celebrities, the striker starred in ads and lent his image to promote products and different types of business. First, there were store inaugurations. Every shop wanted the biggest Brazilian soccer idol to attend their launch as a way of boosting their sales. And Leônidas attended many. He "would waste just ten minutes, enough time to take a photograph and open a bottle of champagne in the inauguration of a shoe shop, [to get paid] a pocket full of gold" (Rodrigues Filho, 2010, p. 221). Because of the 1938 World Cup success, which turned Leônidas into a national celebrity, diverse commercial establishments honored the player and sought to associate their products to his image. These episodes were frequently covered by the press. For instance, newspaper O *Globo* reported about "A gift for Leonidas: the offer from *Fabrica Metallurgica Brasileira*." The text read:

> The brilliant performances of Leonidas in the games that our team played in the Old World, established him as one of the world's most perfect soccer players. This fact generated exceptional enthusiasm in our country, and various stores, excited by the remarkable feat of the 'Black Diamond,' have offered him gifts, which will be delivered when he returns to Rio. *Fabrica Metallurgica Brasileira*, associating itself with these tributes, has just offered the Flamengo player a chrome lamp with a green porcelain spotlight, suitable for an office, which is on display in one of the windows of its store at Rua da Carioca 53.[19]

The tributes paid to the star in exchange for advertising were constant. The report "A royal present for Leonidas: a famous bathroom set of green porcelain offered to the glorious soccer star by the firm J. M. Mello & Cia" informed readers that "The famous 'Hornberg' set was offered to Leonidas in recognition of the great achievements of our glorious 'scorer.'"[20]

Another example was *Paragon* chronograph "by Leonidas."[21] *Jornal dos Sports* reported that:

> Messrs. Coimbra & Fuah, which represent the famous *Paragon* watches in Brazil, offered an expensive *Paragon* chronograph to the player who scored the first goal for Brazil in the 'Copa Roca' competition (...). Leonidas, Flamengo's center forward, won the valuable *Paragon* chronograph, which will be handed to him at the *Jornal dos Sports* office.

In response to all these requests and the constant pressure of companies, Leônidas ended up starring in some ads for stores and brands for free. The soccer star saw no difference between giving his autograph and signing a

132 *Perspectives on consumption (media images)*

paper for a friend asking him for this kind of favor. As a result, he ended up lending his image and/or name to diverse ads without requesting any kind of fee or compensation. On one such occasion, "the entrepreneur Manoel de Brito asked Leônidas to sign a statement saying that he only ate guava paste by *Peixe*. The ad was published in all the newspapers, taking up at least a quarter page" (Ribeiro, 2010, p. 134), and the only payment Leônidas received was a box of guava paste.[22]

At the height of his fame, Leônidas was advised by José Maria Scassa. The journalist explained to the player that giving autographs or writing messages in fan albums was something he could do for free. But featuring in an ad or endorsing a product was work for which he should be duly paid, since the companies were using his image and popularity to make large sums of money. Leônidas not only agreed with Scassa, but invited the journalist to negotiate his advertising contracts. This was the first time that a Brazilian soccer player would be formally hired as a celebrity endorser or official spokesperson for companies, products, and services (Ribeiro, 2010). It was probably at this moment too that agents responsible for negotiating contracts for sports celebrities emerged. One of the first contracts that Leônidas signed was with the Brazilian chocolate company *Lacta*. Soon after the 1938 World Cup, *Lacta* decided to honor the player by launching a new candy bar called *Diamante Negro* (Black Diamond).[23] Like any contemporary celebrity, in this context, the name or nickname of Leônidas was capable of selling anything, including chocolates:

> Ary Silva, present at the meeting, saw the honoree pay money for the use of Leônidas's nickname for one of his chocolates. This detail is important as it shows that use of the *Diamante Negro* label by the chocolate factory was made with the player's consent, even though *Lacta* has frequently been accused of never giving anything to Leônidas. Ary Silva does not know how much money the player was paid. He recalls that some talked about 2 *contos*. But he is certain about one thing. He saw Leônidas receive a 'fistful' of money from the hands of the magnate. The São Paulo journalist also saw Leônidas sign a contract that would entitle him to receive a share of the sales of *Diamante Negro* chocolate.
> (Ribeiro, 2010, p. 135)

In another example, the *Sudan Company*, the country's largest cigarette manufacturer in the 1930s and the 1940s, paid 15 *contos* for the right to name a cigarette brand after Leônidas. On this occasion, the news item "Diamante Negro set out to São Paulo today,"[24] published in *Jornal dos Sports*, reported that the player would receive tributes in the capital of São Paulo and then would head to the city of Campinas, where the business magnate Sabbado D'Angelo would offer him the sponsorship of *Leonidas* cigarettes, created in honor of the star player.[25] During the same period, a watch with his name was launched on the market (Ribeiro, 2010).

A star player in the world of goods   133

These examples reveal that in order to lure consumers, advertising in the 1930s and the 1940s sought to associate products, stores, and brands with the image of Brazil's leading sports celebrity: the striker Leônidas. From the perspective of the anthropology of consumption, we argue that goods create barriers as much as bridges, differences, and similarities, since they bear meanings and can be used as mechanisms both for the inclusion and the exclusion of people and things in certain spaces and groups. Goods construct meanings, enable social relations, and represent identities and lifestyles (Douglas and Isherwood, 1979). Advertising attributes meanings to products and services and introduces them into social life through diverse strategies: one of them involves appropriating the prestige of celebrities and associating their public images to consumer goods (McCracken, 2005), investing in a kind of "prestigious imitation" (Mauss, 1935/1973). Leônidas was the first Brazilian soccer celebrity to participate in that kind of arrangement.

Countless advertisements for products, services and stores, inaugurations, social festivities, and marketing campaigns counted on the soccer player's prestige. The incipient "star system" in Brazil began to include social actors who did not come from the traditional model of the arts, politics, or media. A Black player who was just as popular as President Getúlio Vargas was a significant novelty, something unprecedented in Brazilian society. As a celebrity, Leônidas joined popular names from other areas of expertise, artists, actors, and musicians, like Ary Barroso, Mário Lago, Linda Batista, Paulo Gracindo, Carmen Miranda, Procópio Ferreira, or Grande Otelo, which meant a significant transformation in the market.

Leônidas was someone who did not invent things, but was the catalyzer that made them happen. Three of them stand out clearly in his trajectory. On the pitch, undoubtedly, moments as stunning as the elastic movement of his bicycle kick or the skillful dribbling that transformed the opponent's certainties into an optical illusion. Off the pitch, he catalyzed experiences, identities, and ideologies of Brazilianness for which his body became a canvas and to which his soccer achievements gave consistency and concreteness. In the marketplace, he inaugurated the idea that a specific skill on a particular stage – soccer – could be used to sell things as disparate or paradoxical as cigarettes, watches, or chocolates. Moreover, Leônidas and his circumstances defined a type of space in Brazilian culture – one authorized by the celebrity seal of approval – that ceased to be limited to artists, actors, and singers and became accessible to sports professionals as well. Until Leônidas, there were no sports celebrities. Before him, no money circulated in the sports universe beyond what was obtained from the practice itself, no prestige beyond the small amount offered only by the initiated. After Leônidas, sport in Brazil acquired a new significance as business. Since then, especially today, what was incipient has become responsible for producing all kinds of celebrities and multiple markets that both sustain and are sustained by them.

134 *Perspectives on consumption (media images)*

Notes

1 *Forbes*'s ranking is available at https://www.forbes.com/celebrities/. Last seen February 17, 2021.
2 In Brazil, as in other Latin American countries, in Europe and elsewhere, the sport is called football. Here, we adopt the US name.
3 French newspaper *L'Equipe* named Pelé "athlete of the century" in 1980. Journalists from all over the world voted on the poll that granted the title to the Brazilian player. Jesse Owens, the iconic US track and field athlete, was second on the poll and the Belgium cyclist Eddy Merckx was third.
4 In newspaper reports from the 1930s and the 1940s, the name Leônidas appears without the circumflex accent mark (Leonidas). Despite this fact, we have opted to write his name with an accent as it appears in studies consulted for this article.
5 *O Globo*, January 15, 1934.
6 There was an intense dispute between amateurism and professionalism in the context of Brazilian soccer in the 1930s. As a result, the assemble of the Brazilian national team had to be improvised for the 1934 World Cup.
7 There are numerous explanations for the nickname *Diamante Negro* (Black Diamond). In a statement to the newspaper *Última Hora* in 1964, Leônidas confirmed the idea that the French had coined the nickname after his standout performance in the 1938 World Cup. However, earlier newspaper items, such as an issue of *Jornal dos Sports* published on December 7, 1932, already referred to Leônidas as the Black Diamond.
8 *O Globo*, July 7, 1938.
9 *O Globo*, June 28, 1938.
10 *Molecagem* refers to a kind of children's disobedience and inappropriate behavior that annoys adults but sometimes generates surprising, creative, and funny effects. *Capoeira* is a Brazilian technique developed by the descendants of enslaved Africans that combines combat and dance moves, which are performed to specific music. *Malandragem* refers to the behavior of *malandros*, resourceful, amusing, and bohemian men who bend the laws and rules in their favor.
11 *O Globo*, April 11, 1937.
12 *O Globo*, June 24, 1938.
13 *O Globo*, July 8, 1938.
14 *Jornal dos Sports*, December 10, 1937.
15 *Jornal dos Sports*, October 26, 1937.
16 *Jornal dos Sports*, February 3, 1938
17 *Jornal dos Sports*, July 23, 1938.
18 *O Globo*, July 23, 1938.
19 *O Globo*, July 14, 1938.
20 *O Globo*, August 18, 1938.
21 *Jornal dos Sports*, February 19, 1940.
22 *Peixe* guava paste ad, *Jornal dos Sports*, July 12, 1938.
23 *Diamante Negro* chocolate ad, *O Globo*, December 22, 1938.
24 *Jornal dos Sports*, July 24, 1938.
25 *Leonidas* cigarettes ad, *O Globo*, September 5, 1938.

References

Amaro, F., & Helal, R. (2014). Futebol, corpo e publicidade: um estudo de caso. *Comunicação, Mídia e Consumo*, 11, pp. 139–161.
Araújo, R. A. B. de. (1980). *Os gênios da pelota: Um estudo do futebol como profissão* [Unpublished master's thesis]. Museu Nacional/Universidade Federal do Rio de Janeiro.

A star player in the world of goods   135

Araújo, R. A. B. de. (1994). *Guerra e paz: Casa-Grande & Senzala e a obra de Gilberto Freyre nos anos 30*. Editora 34.

Armstrong, G., & Giulianotti, R. (Eds.). (1999). *Football Cultures and Identities*. Palgrave MacMillan.

Barthes, R. (1957). *Mythologies*. Éditions du Seuil.

Baudrillard, J. (2005). *The System of Objects* (J. Benedict, Trans.). Verso. (Original work published 1968).

Baudrillard, J. (1998). *The Consumer Society: Myths and Structures* (C. Turner, Trans.). Sage Publications. https://www.doi.org/10.4135/9781526401502. (Original work published 1970).

DaMatta, R. (1982). Esporte na sociedade: um ensaio sobre o futebol brasileiro. In: R. DaMatta (Ed.), *Universo do futebol: Esporte e sociedade brasileira* (pp. 19–42). Pinakotheke.

DaMatta, R. (2006). *A bola corre mais que os homens: Duas copas, treze crônicas e três ensaios sobre futebol*. Rocco.

Damo, A. S. (2008). Dom, amor e dinheiro no futebol de espetáculo. *Revista Brasileira de Ciências Sociais*, 23, 139–150.

Damo, A. S. (2009). O simbólico e o econômico no futebol de espetáculo: as estratégias da Fifa para tornar as copas lucrativas a partir de uma interpretação antropológica. *Razón y Palabra*, 69, 1–25.

Damo, A. S. (2011). Produção e consumo de megaeventos esportivos: apontamentos em perspectiva antropológica. *Comunicação, Mídia e Consumo*, 8, 67–92.

Damo, A. S. (2012). Lo econômico e lo simbólico en fútbol mercantilizado: una interpretación antropológica. *Cuadernos de Ciencias Sociales de FLACSO Cuesta Rica*, 160, 71–106.

Damo, A. S., & Oliven, R. G. (2014). *Megaeventos esportivos no Brasil: um olhar antropológico*. Autores Associados.

Douglas, M., & Isherwood, B. (1979). *The World of Goods: Towards an Anthropology of Consumption*. Basic Books.

Duke, V. (1991). The sociology of football: A research agenda for the 1990s. *The Sociological Review*, 39(3), 627–645.

Fausto, B. (2006). *Getúlio Vargas: O poder e o sorriso*. Companhia das Letras.

França, V. (2014). Celebridades: identificação, idealização ou consumo? In: V. França, J. Freire Filho, L. Lana, & P. Guimarães Simões. (Eds.), *Celebridades no século XXI: Transformações no estatuto da fama* (pp. 15–36). Sulina.

Freyre, G. (1938). *Foot-ball* mulato. *Diário de Pernambuco*. Recife, p. 4.

Freyre, G. (1975). *Casa-grande & senzala*. José Olympio. (First published 1933).

Freyre, G. (2010). Prefácio à 1ª edição. In: M. Rodrigues Filho (Ed.), *O negro no futebol brasileiro* (pp. 24–26). Mauad. (First published 1947).

Gastaldo, E. (2002). *Pátria, chuteiras e propaganda: o brasileiro na publicidade da Copa do Mundo*. AnnaBlume.

Gordon, C. (1995). História social dos negros no futebol brasileiro. *Pesquisa de Campo*, 2, 71–90.

Guedes, S. L. (1977). *O futebol brasileiro: Instituição zero* [Unpublished master's thesis]. Museu Nacional/Universidade Federal do Rio de Janeiro.

Helal, R. (1997). *Passes e impasses: Futebol e cultura de massa no Brasil*. Vozes.

Hollanda, B. B. B. de. (2004). *O descobrimento do futebol: modernismo, regionalismo e paixão esportiva em José Lins do Rego*. Biblioteca Nacional.

Hollanda, B. B. B. de. (2010). *O clube como vontade e representação: O jornalismo esportivo e a formação das torcidas organizadas de futebol do Rio de Janeiro*. 7Letras.

136 Perspectives on consumption (media images)

Hughson, J., Moore, K., Spaaij, R., & Maguire, J. (Eds.) (2017). *Routledge Handbook of Football Studies*. Routledge.

Leite Lopes, J. S. (1994). A vitória do futebol que incorporou a pelada. *Revista USP*, 22, 64–83.

Mauss, M. (1973). Techniques of the body (B. Brewster, Trans.). *Economy and Society*, 2(1), 70–88. (Original work published 1935). https://doi.org/10.1080/03085147300000003.

McCracken, G. (1988). *Culture and Consumption: New Approaches to the Symbolic Character of Consumer Goods and Activities*. Indiana University Press.

McCracken, G. (2005). *Culture and Consumption II: Markets, Meaning, and Brand Management*. Indiana University Press.

Miceli, S. (1978). Os Gaviões da Fiel: torcida organizada do Corinthians. *RAE. Revista de Administração de Empresas*, 18(2), 43–46.

Miller, D. (1997). *Capitalism: An Ethnographic Approach*. Berg.

Moeran, B., & Malefyt, T. (2018). *Magical Capitalism: Enchantment, Spells, and Occult Practices in Contemporary Economies*. Palgrave Macmillan.

Mostaro, F., Amaro, F. & Helal, R. (2014). Futebol-arte e consumo: as narrativas presentes na campanha "Ouse ser brasileiro". *Revista Eletrônica do Programa de Pós-Graduação em Mídia e Cotidiano*, 4, 88–104.

Pandolfi, D. (Ed.). (1999). *Repensando o Estado Novo*. Fundação Getulio Vargas.

Pereira, L. A. M. (2000). *Footballmania: uma história social do futebol no Rio de Janeiro, 1902–1938*. Nova Fronteira.

Ribeiro, A. (2010). *Diamante Negro: Biografia de Leônidas da Silva*. Cia. dos Livros.

Rocha, E. (2003). *Jogo de espelhos: Ensaios de cultura brasileira*. Mauad.

Rocha, E. (2006). *Representações do consumo: Estudos sobre a narrativa publicitária*. Mauad.

Rodrigues Filho, M. (2010). *O negro no futebol brasileiro*. Mauad. (First published in 1947).

Rodrigues, José Carlos. (1982). O rei e o rito. *Revista Comum*, 1, 16–29.

Sahlins, M. (1976). *Culture and Practical Reason*. The University of Chicago Press.

Simmel, G. (1904). Fashion. *International Quarterly*, 10, 130–155.

Sodré, M. (1977). Futebol, teatro ou televisão. In: M. Sodré (Ed.), *O monopólio da fala* (pp. 133–155). Vozes.

Sombart, W. (1967). *Luxury and Capitalism* (W. R. Dittmar, Trans.). University of Michigan Press. (Original work published 1913).

Souza, D. A. de. (2008). *O Brasil entra em campo: Construções e reconstruções da identidade nacional (1930–1947)*. Annablume.

Toledo, L. H. de. (1996). *Torcidas organizadas de futebol*. Autores Associados/Anpocs.

Toledo, L. H. de. (2000). *No país do futebol*. Zahar Editor.

Toledo, L. H. de. (2002). *Lógicas no futebol*. Hucitec/Fapesp.

Trentmann, F. (Ed.) (2012). *The Oxford Handbook of the History of Consumption*. Oxford University Press.

Veblen, T. (2007). *The Theory of the Leisure Class*. Oxford University Press. (First published 1899).

Index

Note: Bold page numbers refer to tables; page numbers followed by "n" denote endnotes.

Açҫolini, G. 72
ad agencies 31, 34, 35–36
admen (and women) *see* ad professionals
ad professionals: advertising knowledge and bricolage 8, 17, 42–51; legitimation mechanisms 37–41; professional identity 31–36; research interlocutors (animals in ads research) 17, **19**, 20, 22, 23, 24, 25, 27
advertisements: as an account of history 17; animals in 18, 19, 20, 21–29; classificatory logic 17–18; consumption of 17, 19; dialogue with society 77; gender differences 78; Leônidas da Silva 120, 130, 132, 133; and myths 17, 20, 49–50, 85; setting 20–21; women's magazines 8, 80, 86–87, 89, 90–97, 102–104
advertising: agencies 31, 34, 35–36; and baby names (US) 13; as a classificatory process 15, 16–21, 23, 26, 27, 28, 29, 80, 86; and hedonist bias 2–3; history of 39–40; knowledge 8, 17, 42–51; revenues for media companies 35; sales function 13, 16–17, 33; socioeconomic function of 37–38; sports celebrities 119, 120–121, 128, 130, 131–132, 133; totemism (converting production into consumption) 7, 16, 18, 21–29, 50–51, 85–86, 95, 107–108; ubiquity of 1; women's magazines 8, 77, 86–87, 89, 90–97, 102–104; *see also* ad professionals

alcohol 3, 20, 21, 26, 87, 110, **110**; *see also Campari*; *Smirnoff* vodka ad
Alfredinho (Alfredo Sampaio Filho) 123
animals 15, 18, 19, 20, 21–29
animism 23–24
anthropological approach 2; to advertising 31, 77; consumption studies 6–7, 13; excess of ideas 1; feminine identity 78–79; goods 6, 133; ideological biases 5; society 82–83, 84; *see also* totemism
Appel perfume ad 95
Artemis skincare ad 91
artistic knowledge 42–43, 44

baby names 13–14
Banet-Weiser, S. 14, 78
Barber, K. 19, 104
Barreto, R. M. 48
Barroso, Ary 130
Barthes, Roland 92–93
bazaar world (of white collars) 32, 33–36
beach lifestyle 100–101
beauty ideals 100, 101, 103, 104, 111, 115
beauty products and treatments 3, 78, 90, 91, 92–93, 94, 95
biologism 2, 4–5
Black Diamond (Diamante Negro) *see* da Silva, Leônidas (Diamante Negro/ Black Diamond)
Boa Forma magazine 100, 104–105, 111, **112**, 113, 115n2
body *see* fragmented body
body shapers *see* shapewear

138 *Index*

brands/branding: advertising as classification 18, 20–21, 26, 27, 86; advertising setting 20–21; anthropomorphism 22–23; baby names 13–14; humanizing products 22–23; market position 27; sports celebrities 119, 120; vodka advertisements 18
Brazil: beach lifestyle 100–101; cultural identity 125, 127, 128, 133; Estado Novo (New State) dictatorship 125; re-democratization (1980s) 8, 77–78, 88–89, 97; traditional values 102; *see also* Terena people
bricolage: and advertising knowledge 8, 17, 42–51; thinking in primitive cultures 107
Brito, Manoel de 132
Budweiser 18
Bulcão, Argemiro 126

Campari 27
capitalism: axis of Western modernity 61, 62, 64, 65; consumption's importance to 1, 13; magazine representations of women 78; moralist bias 3; Terena people 8, 55–56, 60, 65, 66–73; *see also* production
Cardoso de Oliveira, Roberto 55, 56, 57, 58, 59, 68, 72
Carnival celebrations 102
cars 3, 18
celebrities *see* sports celebrities
Chickasaw people 106, 109–110
Chique perfume ad 90
cigarette advertising and promotion 24, 25, 27, 130, 132
classification 84–85; advertising as a classificatory process 15, 16–21, 23, 26, 27, 28, 29, 80, 86; consumption's powers of 3, 7, 8, 16, 21; gender 78, 80; indigenous populations (grades of contact) 59–60, 64; social identities 80, 81–84; *see also* totemism
Clastres, Pierre 53–54, 61–62, 63–64
Claudia magazine 87, 100, 103, 104, 105, 109–110, **110**, 113, 114, 115n2
clothes 16, 90, 91, 94–95; *see also* shapewear
Coca-Cola 22
college education 38–39
communication schools 38, 39, 41

Compare the Market 18
consumer culture theory 7
consumption: of advertisements 17, 19; advertising as a pillar of 13; anthropological approach 7, 13, 15; and capitalism 1, 13; the case for academic attention 1–2, 4; conversion from production by advertising 7, 16, 18, 21–29, 50–51, 85–86, 95, 107–108; cultural perspective, history of 6–7; female body in pieces 89, 91, 95, 97; ideological biases 1, 2–6; ideology of 14, 49–50, 85, 100, 101–102; by indigenous people 57, 66; and the media system 79; self-actualization through 14, 78; and soccer stars 8, 119, 120, 121, 130–133; target audience 19; totemic logic in women's magazines 100, 101, 105, 108–115; totemic temporality 79, 100, 101, 110–113, **112**; use of female body images 78; by young women 78
copywriting 38, 40, 42, 44
corsets 103
cosmetics 3, 78, 90, 91, 92–93, 94, 95
Costa, Flávio 123, 125
creative directors 42
creativity 8, 17, 20, 42, 46, 47–48, 49, 51
cultural identity: Brazilian soccer 125, 127, 128, 133; indigenous people 8, 53, 55, 56, 60, 61; *see also* feminine identity
culture: advertising-assigned meanings *see* totemism; Brazilian identity 125, 127, 128, 133; feminine bodies 104 (*see also* feminine identity); gender differences in advertisements 78; hedonism 2–3; indigenous ethnic identity 53, 55, 56, 60, 61; industry of 1–2, 79–80; mass media as an active voice of 79; naturalism 23; public nature of 19, 80; social identity 77, 84; studies on 6–7, 14–15; symbolic order 5

Dahrendorf, Ralph 81, 82, 83
DaMatta, R. 28, 82–83, 102
Del Rio lingerie ad 90
DeMillus shapewear ads 91, 93–94, 103
democracy *see* re-democratization (1980s)

Index 139

Descola, P. 23
determinism *see* biologism
Diamante Negro (Black Diamond) *see*
   da Silva, Leónidas (Diamante Negro/
   Black Diamond)
Diamante Negro chocolate 8, 120, 132
diets *see* weight management
Douglas, M. 6, 7, 85
dramatized knowledge 40, 43
Dropnyl ad 95
DuLoren ad 90, 95
Dumont, L. 62
Durkheim, E. 80

economic knowledge 44
economic production *see* production
Eco, Umberto 1
education: for ad professionals 38–39,
   41; socioeconomic function of
   advertising 38
engineer's logic 49, 107
Esso ads 24
Estado Novo (New State)
   dictatorship 125
ethnic identity 53, 55, 56, 60, 61
ethnocentrism 54, 65
ethnocide 54–55, 58, 61, 62, 64, 65, 66,
   72, 73

Fabrica Metallurgica Brasileira 131
Fatal Attraction (film) 89
Faustinho, Jarbas (Jarbas) 122, 123
Fausto ("Black Marvel") 123, 129
feminine identity: and Brazilian
   beach lifestyle 100; and Brazilian
   re-democratization (1980s) 8, 77–78,
   81, 87–89, 97; fragmented body 77,
   80, 81, 89, 90–97, 101; and men 78,
   90; notes on method 86–89
feminism 78, 89, 97, 101
Ferreira, Procópio 130
Filho, Alfredo Sampaio
   (Alfredinho) 123
Filho, Mário (Rodrigues) 126–127, 128,
   129, 130, 131
football *see* soccer
Football World Cup (1934) 123
Football World Cup (1938) 124,
   129, 130
Forbes magazine 119
fragmented body: body parts connected
   to specific goods 101, 104, 105,
   108–109, 113, 114; feminine identity

77, 80, 81, 89, 90–97, 101; self-
   actualization journeys 14
França, V. 128
Freud, Sigmund 1, 6
Freyre, Gilberto 102, 103, 127
Frito-lay's Cheetos 18

Geertz, Clifford 19, 80
general knowledge 45–46
genocide 54, 55, 64, 73
Goffman, E. 41, 78, 81–82
Gordon, C. 123, 126
Gradim, Oscarino 122
Graeber, D. 8n1
Guaná nation 57, 58; *see also* Terena
   people
The Guardian (newspaper ad) 18
da Guia, Domingos 122, 123,
   127, 129

happiness 2–3, 14, 85, 101, 103, 104
Hardin, M. 78
"Health" ("Saúde", *Claudia* magazine)
   105, 109–110, **110**, 114
hedonism 2–3
Helena Rubinstein 92
Hidraskin ad 92
historical appropriation 39–40
historicism, axis of Western modernity
   61, 62, 63, 65
history, told by advertisements 17
Hopkins, Claude 33, 43
Hughes, E. 38, 39

idealized life 3, 14, 49–50, 51, 78, 85,
   100, 103
identity: ad professionals 31–36; baby
   names 13; and Brazilian soccer 125,
   127, 128, 133; indigenous people
   8, 53, 55, 56, 60, 61; individualism
   and social fact 80, 82–84; male 80;
   moralist bias 3; product personality
   22; through consumption 1, 13, 14,
   86; *see also* feminine identity
ideological biases 1–6
ideology: Brazil's cultural diversity
   125, 128, 133; of capitalism 50; of
   consumption 2–3, 14, 49–50, 51,
   79, 85, 100, 101–102; ideological
   biases 1–6; ideological universe 79;
   individualism 83; media portrayal of
   women 78, 100, 103–104, 105
Indian Protection Service (SPI) 58–59

140   Index

indigenous people: and axes of Western modernity 63–64; Chickasaw 106, 109–110; contact, grades of 59–60, 64; ethnocide 54–55, 58, 61, 62, 64, 65, 66, 72, 73; government policy 53–54; *see also* Terena people
individualism: axis of Western modernity 56, 61, 62, 65, 83, 84; moralist condemnation 3
individuality 78, 80, 82–83, 90–97, 103
intellectual world (of white collars) 32
internships 40–41
invariance 100, 105
Isherwood, B. 6, 7

Jarbas (Jarbas Faustinho) 122, 123
J. M. Mello & Cia 131
Jornal dos Sports 123, 126, 130, 131, 132, 134n7

kaleidoscope metaphor 46, 48, 49
Kates, S. M. 78
Kellog's Frosted Flakes 18
Kilbourne, J. 78
Kinikináu people 58
knowledge: and bricolage 8, 17, 42–51; dramatized 40, 43

Lacta (Diamante Negro chocolate) 8, 120, 132
Leach, Edmund 83
legitimation mechanisms 37–41
Leonidas cigarettes 132
Lévi-Strauss, Claude: bricolage 17, 46–47, 48, 49, 107; mythical thought 20, 49, 106; primitive societies 63, 106, 107, 108; social identities 84; and totemic logic in women's magazines 101, 108, 114; totemic organization 7, 15, 16, 18, 23, 50, 84–85, 101; totemic temporality 79, 85, 101, 114
Lib Slip ad 91
Lipmaker ad 95
liquor 3, 20, 26, 87, 110, **110**; *see also* *Campari*; *Smirnoff* vodka ad
living standard (of ad professionals) 37
Lopes, J. 13
Lynn, S. 78

McChad jeans ad 91
magazines: and the ad industry 35; *Forbes* 119; niche 19; novelty 100, 114; sporting celebrities 120, 121, 124, 128; sports magazines 78; *see also* women's magazines
magical thought 7, 8, 23, 106, 113, 115; *see also* mythical thought
magical time (totemic temporality) 79, 85, 100, 101, 107, 110–113, **112**, 114, 115
Magnólia cigarettes 130
Malanga, E. 39–40, 43
Malu Mulher (TV show) 89
managerial world (of white collars) 32
Marinho, Roberto 126
Marx, Karl 16, 21, 86, 107
mass media: advertising revenues 35; collective representations 80; ideological universe 79; magic system of 107; moralist narratives 4; representation of women 77, 78, 101, 104 (*see also* women's magazines); television 14, 19, 35, 42, 80, 88, 89, 128; under Brazil's military regime 88; *see also* newspapers; sporting press
Match magazine 124
Matitte jeans ad 90
Max Factor ads 90, 92, 95
Mbayá-Guaicuru people 57
media *see* mass media
men: ads aimed at 91, 94; media representation 78, 79, 80, 90; traditional values 102
Mercedes-Benz 18
Merckx, Eddy 134n3
Messi, Lionel 119
"Me Too" movement 77
modernity *see* Western modernity
moralism 2, 3–4
Mundo Esportivo 126
mythical thought 36, 49–50, 51, 106; *see also* magical thought
myths 17, 20, 37, 49–50, 85

naming: babies 13–14; products 21–22
naturalism 23
nature: animals in advertisements 24; animals as part of 18; animism 23; natural body 96, 108; naturalism 23; totemism 15–16, 23, 50, 85, 106, 108–109
newspapers 35, 79, 80, 88; soccer celebrities 8, 120, 121, 123, 126, 128–132, 134n7
Neymar (Neymar da Silva Santos Júnior) 119

Index   141

NOB (Northwest railroad of Brazil) 58
Nova magazine 87, 90, 100, 104, 105, 108–109, **109**, **110**, 111, 113, 115n2

office world (of white collars) 32
Ogilvy, David 37, 47–48
O Globo 126, 128, 129, 131
O Globo Esportivo 126
old professional world (of white collars) 32
Owens, Jesse 134n3

Padilha, Bastos 128
Paragon watches 131
Paraguayan War (1864–1870) 57
patriarchy 78, 102
Pelé (Edson Arantes do Nascimento) 119
Pereira, L. A. M. 122, 123, 124, 125, 126–127
perfume ads 90, 95
Phillips, E. B. 79
Portuguese empire 57, 62
Portwood-Stacer, L. 14, 78
Power Bust Flex ad 91–92
primitive societies 61–62, 63–64, 106, 107, 108
production: academic interest 1, 4; conversion into consumption (totemism) 7, 16, 18, 21–29, 50–51, 85–86, 95, 107–108; Marx on 16, 21, 86, 107; moralist bias 3–4; primitive societies 63–64; protestant work ethic 72; State society 54, 62; Terena people and capitalist norms 8, 55–56, 58, 60, 65, 66–73; Western modernity 62, 63–64
product launch 22
professional roles 82
Protestantism 72
psychoanalysis 1, 6
psychology: advertisements 18, 43, 80; idealized lives 101; identity as social fact 80; ideological biases (consumption study) 1, 4, 5; knowldge of (ad professionals) 42, 44, 45, 46

Quadros, Jânio 88

Rabelo, Genival 37
racism 119–120, 121, 123, 126, 127
radio 19, 35, 80, 88, 120, 121, 126, 128
Rede Globo 89

re-democratization (1980s) 8, 77–78, 88–89, 97
remuneration (ad professionals) 37
Ribeiro, A. 122, 123, 124, 128, 129, 130, 131, 132
Ribeiro, Darcy 59, 60, 64–65, 73
Rio Branco Cup (1932) 122, 129
Rio championship (1935) 123
ritualization 28, 111
Rocha, E. 7, 16–20, 54, 79, 87, 107
Rodrigues Filho, Mário 126–127, 128, 129, 130, 131
roles *see* social identities
Ronaldo, Christiano 119
Rondon Commission: Marshal Rondon 58

Sahlins, Marshall 7, 16, 21, 64, 106
salaries (of ad professionals) 37
sales: advertising function 13, 16–17, 33
salespeople 32–35, 70
Sanny ad 94–95
Sant'Anna, A. 38, 43, 45
Santos, Fausto dos (Fausto, "Black Marvel") 123, 129
Sapataria Capital 131
savage thought 106
Scassa, José Maria 131, 132
scientific knowledge 42–43
self-actualization 3, 14, 78
self-improvement 104, 109, 111, 114
"Sexy Portion" ("Porção Sexy", *Nova* magazine) 105, 109, **110**, 113, 114
Shakespeare, William (*As You Like It*) 82
shapewear 91, 93–94, 103–104
Shaw-Garlock, G. 78
Sigvaris Sculptor ad 103
Silva, Ary 132
da Silva, Leônidas (Diamante Negro/ Black Diamond): career summary 121–125; celebrity status 8, 120, 121, 124, 128–131; environment of racial discrimination 119–120, 126; and the rhthym of Brazilian soccer 127, 128; soccer and consumption 8, 119, 121, 130–133
Skin Dew ad 92
Smirnoff vodka ad 17–18
soccer 121, 123; professionalization 123, 125–126; sporting media expansion 126; and state 125; *see also* da Silva, Leônidas (Diamante Negro/Black Diamond)

142 Index

Soccer World Cup (1934) 123
Soccer World Cup (1938) 124, 129, 130
social identities 77, 78, 80, 81–84; *see also* cultural identity
social relationships 1, 6, 18, 21, 27–29, 86, 133
social sciences: 1980s Brazil 89; advertising knowledge 42, 44, 45; on the body 108; on consumption 1, 4; gender-based study 89; identity and classification 81; role and status 81
socioeconomic function of advertising 37–38
sociological knowledge of 42, 44, 45
Souza, D. A. 123, 124, 125, 126
SPI *see* Indian Protection Service (SPI)
spirit: biologism 4; ethnocide 54, 55; female individuality 94, 95, 96, 97
sporting press 78, 121, 123, 124, 126–127, 128, 130, 134n7; *see also Jornal dos Sports*; *O Globo*
sports celebrities 8, 119; *see also* da Silva, Leônidas (Diamante Negro/ Black Diamond)
State: axis of Western modernity 61–62, 63, 64, 65; and soccer 125
Sudan Company 132
Sulfabril ad 95
Swanton, John R. 106
symbolism: advertising 2, 8, 21, 80, 86; anthropological tradition 77, 78–79; consumption 1, 4, 5, 6–7, 8, 13, 15, 21, 23; production 16, 107; totemism 15

"Target Shot" ("Tiro ao Alvo", *Nova* magazine) 105, 108–109, **109**, 113, 114
television 14, 19, 35, 42, 80, 88, 89, 128
temporality, totemic 79, 85, 100, 101, 107, 110–113, **112**, 114, 115
Terena, Cisto 69–71
Terena, Luís 53, 54, 55, 69, 71
Terena people: and capitalist norms 8, 55–56, 60, 65, 66–73; ethnic identity 53, 55, 56, 61; integration of 56–60, 65; land of 53, 54, 55; religion 72
Terena reservation 53, 54, 55, 66
Terra dos Índios (Vianna) 54–55
theater metaphor 81–82

Thoumazeau, Raymond 124
time, totemic 79, 85, 100, 101, 107, 110–113, **112**, 114, 115
totemism: advertising (converting production into consumption) 7, 16, 18, 21–29, 50–51, 85–86, 95, 107–108; logic in women's magazines 100, 101, 105, 108–115; nature/ culture conversion 15–16, 23, 50, 85, 106, 108–109; time 79, 85, 100, 101, 107, 110–113, **112**, 114, 115
tribal societies *see* indigenous people
TV Mulher (TV show) 89

underwear ads 90, 91, 93–94, 103
universalism: and biologism 4, 5
utilitarianism 2, 5–6

Vargas, Getúlio 122, 125, 129, 133
Velho, G. 32, 61
Vianna, Zelito (*Terra dos Índios*) 54–55
vodka *see Smirnoff* vodka ad

Walsdorf, K. 78
wealth (of ad professionals) 37
weight management 108–109, 111–113, **112**, 114
Wella's Kolestral cream ad 94
Western modernity 56, 61–65, 83, 84, 105–106
white collar worlds 32, 33; *see also* bazaar world (of white collars)
Williams, Raymond 107
women: Brazil's re-democratization 8, 77–78, 89, 97; Carnival celebrations 102; traditional values 102; *see also* feminine identity; women's magazines
women's magazines 104–105; advertisements in 8, 77, 86–87, 89, 90–97, 102–104; ideological consequences of the portrayal of women 78; totemic logic 100, 101, 105, 108–115
work, Terena people's view of 56, 59, 60, 63–64, 65, 67–68, 70–71, 72
World Cup (1934) 123
World Cup (1938) 124, 129, 130
Wright Mills, C. 32

Young, J. W. 48

Printed in the United States
by Baker & Taylor Publisher Services